FIGHT
The Good Fight
A Battle Plan for Life

Spencer H. Silverglate, Esq.

Copyright © 2010 Spencer Silverglate Esq.
All rights reserved.

Permission to reproduce or transmit any portion of this book in any form or by any means must be obtained by contacting Spencer H. Silverglate at ssilverglate@csclawfirm.com.

ISBN: 1450548865
ISBN-13: 9781450548861

Cover Design: Kat Silverglate

For Cameron

Dear Pat,

I hope you and Susie enjoy this book as much as I have. I've come to realize the most important Leave inheritance we can about life. Our children is about God's purpose in their life and their eternal destiny when our life journey is over.

All God's Blessings & Prayers on your marriage and family,

Kenny

November 2010

Acknowledgements

My heartfelt appreciation goes to all those who impacted this project.

First and foremost, I thank you God for using an imperfect vessel like me to share your call to action.

To my wife Kat, the love of my life. You are my biggest supporter. All of the ideas in the book were either inspired or refined by our shared experiences and countless discussions.

To my son Cameron, thank you for listening to my endless stories and lectures. Your unwarranted admiration inspires me to become the man you think I am.

Thank you to my friends and family who provided their insight, guidance and encouragement: Win Green, Frank Ramos, Mike Montgomery, Tom Turpin, Eric Stewart, Ken Johnson, Joanem Floreal, Russell Silverglate, Scot Silverglate, Joe Ankus and Jay Gayoso.

I am indebted to all the amazing preachers and authors who have shaped my worldview. Among them are Win Green, Stan Telchin, Andy Stanley, John Maxwell, John Eldridge, Robert Lewis, Rick Warren, John Ortberg, C.S. Lewis, Stephen Covey and Victor Frankl.

I am grateful to my parents Barney and Gertrude Silverglate. You gave me life and set my feet on the right path. I hope you're smiling in heaven.

Contents

Introduction	1
Lesson One	19
It's Not About You	
Lesson Two	29
You Can Live Without Anything — Except Purpose	
Lesson Three	43
Life is Hard — Choose to Fight	
Lesson Four	65
Character is What You Do When No One is Looking	
Lesson Five	85
Most of Life is About Showing Up	
Lesson Six	101
Whatever You Choose to Do, Do it with All Your Heart	
Lesson Seven	119
Worldly Pursuits Will Never Satisfy You Completely	
Lesson Eight	139
You Were Destined for Greatness	
Lesson Nine	159
You Were Born to Love	
Lesson Ten	181
Life is a Journey, Not a Destination	
Epilogue	199

Introduction

The water fired out of the shower faucet in slow motion, one painful drop at a time. Surely I was drowning, yet helpless to do anything about it. I searched my memory for his advice; some credo or something that my father must have taught me about life. All I could remember was "don't volunteer if you're in the Army." But I wasn't in the Army. I was in a shower, fully clothed; the oxygen being squeezed from my lungs. The walls were closing in. Reality set in.

Dad was dead.

I was an 18 year-old college freshman and had just received a call in my dorm room that my father had died. As of that moment, I was an orphan, my mother having died four years earlier. Life as I knew it was over.

I'm 45 today, and as I reflect back, most of my life has been a fight. At least, that's the way I see it. Not a physical fight, but a struggle in one way or another. I'm happy to report that my life did not end that day in 1981 when I got the call that dad died. I faced a choice though. Would I stand and fight, as my parents would have wanted, or would I become bitter and give up?

To me, one of the overarching questions in life is not whether we will face challenges and hardship. We all will. The question is how we respond to them. Will we fight? If so, for whom will we fight? For what will we stand? And by what principles will we live?

The purpose of this book is to answer these questions for myself and to record them for you Cameron, my only child. The book is written in first person directly from me to you. Since I lost my parents when I wasn't much older than you are now, I feel a sense of urgency to pass on something of what I've learned over the past 45 years. I desperately wish I had this from my parents. I learned so much from them, but on the big questions, they were mostly silent. What did they think about life and death? About God? About our purpose here on earth? We never seemed to talk about these things.

My goal is to make sure that you won't be asking these same questions about me when you're an adult. When I exist only as a faded picture in a photo album, I don't want there to be any ambiguity about the values I held dear.

When you were two-years-old, I started keeping a journal of the significant events in our lives and the lessons I was learning from them. This book is basically a synopsis of that journal, boiled down to the ten most important life lessons. I view them as a battle plan for life. But to understand the lessons, I first need to tell you my story.

My Parents

Both my maternal and paternal lineage is Jewish as far back as anyone in my family can remember. I am the youngest of three sons—the baby as my dad would say. My brother Scot is three years older than me. My brother Larry is 28 years older. Growing up, I received the typical religious training for a reformed Jewish boy, culminating in a bar mitzvah at age 13. Like many reformed Jews, my religious experience was mostly cultural.

I had two wonderful and loving parents (your grandparents) whom I miss even as I write this. They were everything to me. My dad Barney was born in 1913. He fancied himself as a tough guy from Brooklyn. He was really a push-over with a gigantic heart. He dropped out of school as a youngster to help support his family and never went back. By the time he was my age now, he was married, widowed and had already lost a daughter to cancer. Larry was his only surviving child.

Then along came Gertrude. She was a 39 year-old career woman in the 1950's who was on a trajectory to remain unmarried for life. That was until she met Barney. It was love at first sight, and the unlikely couple married within weeks.

When I was born, my mom was already 43, and my dad was 50. To make matters worse, their health was horrible. They were old-school—overweight, under-exercised, smokers. My mom had breast cancer and lung cancer. My dad had heart disease and diabetes. Many of my childhood memories involve hospitals—my mother's mastectomy, my father's open heart surgery and leg amputation, my mother's radiation and chemotherapy.

I can remember my father undergoing an operation at New York University Hospital to improve the circulation in his left leg. It appeared as if the operation was successful. I went to synagogue that evening to thank God for what seemed like a miracle. The next day, his leg was amputated. Seemingly overnight, my mother's cancer took a turn for the worse. Again, I prayed for a miracle, but none came. She died six months later. I was 14 (your age now).

Much of my father's will to live died with my mother. Yet he was determined to see me off to college. With the aid of medical science and, I now believe, divine intervention, he made it. He lived barely long enough to see me back out of the driveway in my Plymouth Trail Duster and head north for the University of Florida. A month later, I got the call that he had died.

INTRODUCTION

My Love

I was now 18 years old with no parents, no money and few prospects. I couldn't understand why God had forsaken me. Then on September 11, 1982, everything changed. That was the day I met my future wife, your mother, the only woman that I have ever loved, Kathy "Kat" Clark.

We met at a fraternity party during the spring semester of our sophomore year. Kat was 18, I was 19. While the other kids were partying and carrying on, Kat and I were talking about life and death, about God and the meaning of it all. Like me, she had a tough childhood. Her father Bruce committed suicide when she was just 10 years old. She was raised by her Irish immigrant mother in Atlantic Beach, Florida. Kat had a Catholic upbringing, but I would call her a nominal Catholic. She was filled with the spirit, but not the doctrine. She certainly had no compunctions about dating and later marrying a Jewish boy like me.

Yet there was something different about this Kathy Clark. She had both gravitas and grace. She had beauty and intelligence. She was Grace Kelly, Katherine Hepburn and my mother all rolled into one. But most of all, she had a light shining on the inside that attracted everyone with whom she came in contact. It wasn't until later that I learned that the light had a name. It was Jesus Christ.

Shortly after we began dating, Kat got sick—real sick. She would faint everywhere—on our way to class, during class, in restaurants. She was diagnosed with a subdural hematoma—a blood clot in her head, pressing on her brain. The doctors never figured out where it came from. But it had to come out or she would die. Kat's head was shaved, and she was rushed in for emergency brain surgery. While her life was flashing before her eyes, so was mine. After living 18 years with sick parents, I wondered if I was cursed—if I was meant to live my entire life dealing with sickness and death. Some of my well-meaning advisors counseled me to cut and run. I'm happy to say that I never seriously entertained that thought, and Kat made a full recovery.

Both Kat and I went on to finish college and then law school at the University of Florida. We financed our educations through work, social security benefits, scholarships and student loans. Upon graduation in 1988, we got married and moved to Miami where we started our careers as civil litigation attorneys.

My Career

I began my legal career with a large, international law firm. The firm was fine, but God really smiled on me when he paired me with my mentor, Mercer "Bud" Clarke (no relation to Kat). Bud is a lawyer's lawyer—brilliant, but with a healthy dose of homespun pragmatism. I handed my resumé to Bud 20 years ago and haven't given it to another employer since. Bud taught me how to be a lawyer. In 1993, we started our own firm, Clarke & Silverglate, P.A.

As a trial lawyer for the past 20 years, I've had my share of courtroom battles and litigation scuffles. Along the way, I also trained in martial arts and earned a black belt in Ju Jitsu. These experiences, together with my growing resumé of real life trials and tribulations, taught me to be a fighter.

My Son

"Low FSH levels," the doctor told Kat. "That's why you're not getting pregnant. Your hormone levels are low." More obstacles. We (the royal we) endured expensive, lengthy, painful, humiliating infertility treatments. Then one day we got the news. Kat was pregnant. A later sonogram revealed it was a boy. And on March 19, 1995, you were born Cameron.

But not without a fight.

During childbirth, your umbilical cord wrapped around your neck, constricting and choking you with every contraction. Your heart rate monitor echoed throughout the delivery room, slowing with every successive beat.

Thump . . thump . . . . . thump . . . . thump . . . . thump.

It was way too late to deliver you by C-Section. You had to be sucked out with a vacuum device attached to your head. You were born with meconium in your lungs. There was high drama. You came into this world fighting, right from the start. But by the grace of God, everything eventually turned out alright. You became a healthy baby and child.

I learned from that experience that you don't just love your kids; you fall in love with them. During your struggle for life on your very first day, I fell in love with you, Cameron.

Years later, after several miscarriages, Kat suffered a ruptured fallopian tube. She would never bear children again. You are our one and only child.

My Salvation

"We can celebrate the Jewish holidays and have a bar mitzvah for Cameron if that's what you want," Kat offered. She knew that my Jewish roots were important to me even though I couldn't articulate why. The truth is, I didn't know what I wanted to teach you about God and religion. I didn't know what I believed myself. My Jewish upbringing seemed to leave me with more questions than answers. So in 1997, when you were two-years-old, I embarked on a spiritual journey of sorts. At the same time, I started your journal. My very first entry is a window into what I was feeling at the time:

Introduction

5/7/97

Cameron:

My 34th birthday was yesterday. The night before, I watched the biography of Andrew Carnegie on public TV. He was an industrialist in the late 1800's who owned steel mills. His story seems to epitomize the conflict in all men—the desire to do good on the one hand and for worldly success on the other. He expressed both desires in large measure.

Carnegie was 33 (my age) when he wrote himself a letter, promising that he would work only two more years because he found the pursuit of money "degrading to the soul." During those 48 months, he made two discoveries that would determine the course of his life. First, he read the works of Herbert Spencer (of all names), an economist who espoused a survival of the fittest economic theory. Second, he discovered a new technology for converting iron into steel.

The two years turned into 32 years, and Carnegie became one of the richest Americans ever. He was ruthless in his pursuit of wealth, but his later years were marked by great philanthropy. He ultimately gave away almost all of his money to charity.

   I find Carnegie's story so compelling because it's my story too. Okay, maybe I haven't attained his level of worldly success, but the good and not-so-good forces that lived in him are alive in me. I am 34 and the managing partner of a law firm. By worldly standards, I'm a success. I even like my job. The only thing I don't like is that I'm away from you and mom 11 hours a day. Hey, maybe I'll work for only two more years like Carnegie, huh?

   How many people who are really succeeding in life give it up to pursue a higher purpose? I'd like to believe that if and when that purpose if ever made clear to me, your father would be such a person.

   I've decided to start this journal today to take you along on my journey. I hope it will have a different meaning for you at different stages in your life. But I caution you not to take it as the gospel. I'm just a man; I'll leave the gospel to God.

Love,

Dad

I began my spiritual journey like any lawyer would—by gathering evidence. I started by reading the Bible, both Old and New Testaments. But I didn't stop there. I read every religious book I could get my hands on. I attended houses of worship ranging from Buddhist and Unitarian to Messianic and Pentecostal—and everything in between. I spoke with religious leaders of every stripe. Finally, after an 18-month search, I boiled my questions down to four:[1]

1. Do I believe in God?

2. If so, is it the God of the Old Testament?

3. If so, does the Old Testament prophesy a messiah?

4. If so, is Jesus Christ the messiah?

---

[1] The book Betrayed had a particularly big impact on my thinking. Stan Telchin, *Betrayed* (Michigan: Chosen Books, 2004).

My answer to the first question was relatively easy. From the time I was a child, I knew God existed—despite my suffering. And while I had the occasional doubts, I always returned to God. When I learned about the big bang theory, my first thought was, "Who caused the bang?" If one day there was nothing, and the next, something, who set the events in motion? To me, it was the proverbial no-brainer. Not to mention the evidence of a creator all around us. The order of the universe. The planets. The earth. The mountains. The oceans. A butterfly's wing. A human eye. Love. Hope. The birth of a child.

You, Cameron.

Yes, God exists.

For me, the answer to the second question also came naturally. Being raised a Jew, the one thing I did know was that there is only one God for all people and for all time—the Lord of lords and King of kings, The Great I Am. This is the God of the Old Testament.

During my year-and-a-half of study, I focused on the messianic prophesies throughout the Old Testament—the prediction that at a messiah would come and save the world. There is no serious debate that Judaism is a messianic religion.

The question, then, is who is the messiah?

INTRODUCTION

The Old Testament predicts that the messiah will descend from the line of King David,[2] be born of a virgin,[3] in Bethlehem,[4] and will be called Immanuel ("God with us").[5] The Book of Isaiah, written 700 years before Christ, foretells the messiah's earthly mission:

> But he was pierced for our transgressions, he was crushed for our iniquities; the punishment that brought us peace was upon him, and by his wounds we are healed. We all, like sheep, have gone astray, each of us has turned to his own way; and the Lord has laid on him the iniquity of us all.
>
> * * *
>
> For he bore the sin of many, and made intercession for the transgressors.[6]

Sound like anyone you know? If I said I am the messiah, you could prove a hundred ways to Sunday that I'm not. But Jesus said he is the messiah, and no one could prove him wrong. He performed countless miracles. He healed the sick. He raised the dead. He walked on water

---

[2] Isaiah 7:14.
[3] Isaiah 7:14.
[4] Micah 5:2.
[5] Isaiah 7:14.
[6] Isaiah 53:5-12.

and turned it into wine. He even predicted his own death and resurrection.

But why did Jesus have to die?

The Old Testament teaches that God is holy. And since man's fall from grace in the Garden of Eden, we've all had to live apart from God. Sin separates us from God. As it turns out, we all have a sin nature (not just me and my buddy Andrew Carnegie). In the words of the Prophet Isaiah, "We all like sheep have gone astray." In other words, none of us is good—not one.

So what's a sinner to do?

In Old Testament times, every breach of the law required some type of sacrifice, frequently a blood sacrifice. Sometimes a bird, other times a goat, calf, bull or lamb—always perfect and without blemish. When major sin was committed, blood had to be spilled.

But we don't sacrifice animals anymore, so what changed?

In the Book of Genesis, God commanded Abraham to kill his only son Isaac. At the last minute, an angel of the Lord interceded and provided a ram as a substitute sacrifice—foreshadowing how God intended to bridge the gulf of sin separating himself from man. It would require no ordinary sacrifice, but the mother of all sacrifices. Or the son as it turned out.

Introduction

The words of the Old Testament became flesh when God created a son in the form of Jesus Christ, the messiah, whose purpose was to come to earth to die for our sins. To be the last sacrifice. Like the lamb whose blood was smeared on the doorposts of the houses during the first Passover, Jesus was innocent of any crime. Yet he was tried, convicted and crucified. But in three days, he rose from the dead.

But did Jesus really rise from the dead?

Not one, but hundreds witnessed Jesus completely dead and, a few days later, fully alive. Not only that, there would have been intense interest to find Jesus' corpse. The Roman government would have wanted to quell civil unrest, and the religious establishment would have wanted to prove that Christ was not the messiah. Yet his corpse was never found. That's because there was no corpse. Jesus Christ rose from the dead and ascended into heaven, where he is today, sitting at the right hand of God.

On the cross, Jesus conquered death itself—not just for the Jews but for everyone and for all time. If we simply confess our sins and put our faith in him, we too will have eternal life: "For God so loved the world that he gave his one and only Son, that whoever believes in him shall not perish but have eternal life."[7]

---

[7] John 3:16.

I came to understand that I am a sinner and that my good works will never be good enough to save me. The *only* way to salvation is through faith in Jesus Christ. Salvation is found in no one else.[8] We are saved in Christ alone.[9] The only way to the Father is through the Son.[10]

I can assure you, I arrived at this conclusion not because it was convenient. There was nothing convenient about admitting to my Jewish relatives and lifelong Jewish friends that I was now a Christian. Nor did I make this decision for my wife Kat. Those who know me will attest that I'm not that nice.

I reached this conclusion for one reason and one reason only—I believe it to be the truth. I can't fully explain it, but something changed in me when I accepted Christ. I became a new creation, one with a purpose. I had a leader and a Lord whom I could trust and follow.

Looking back on my life, I can see that the events that brought me to the point of belief were not accidental. The struggles and hardships that Kat and I endured growing up led us inexorably to each other. They formed the common ground that bonded us together. Family illnesses, deaths and almost unbearable tragedies were redeemed in love. After more tribulations

---

[8] Acts 4:12.
[9] Romans 10:9.
[10] John 14:6.

and long odds, we had you, Cameron, our only child. And in searching for your salvation, I found my own.

On September 13, 1998—ten years ago to the day that I'm writing this—both you and I were baptized into the body of believers. In one sense, my spiritual journey was completed, but in another, it was just beginning. I continue on that journey today.

Cameron, more important than anything on the pages that follow, I want you to know that God exists. And the answer to every question is found in his son Jesus Christ. He is the hope of the world. He will make you more than a conqueror.[11] You can do all things in Christ who strengthens you.[12] This is the most important lesson of all. If you don't embrace this foundational truth—if you don't accept Jesus Christ as Lord and savior—everything else is meaningless. He is the way and the truth and the life.[13]

But alas, the choice is yours. You'll have your own roads to travel as you journey through life. You'll have to draw your own conclusions. The journey will be hard at times. Life can bring you to your knees, son. But the battle is worth it. It's definitely worth it.

---

[11] Romans 8:37.
[12] Philippians 4:13.
[13] John 14:6.

So if you ever find yourself drowning in self-pity, struggling for what do next, you'll never have to wonder what my advice would be.

Fight.

Lesson O

It's Not About You

"The world does not revolve around you."

—Gertrude Silverglate (my mother)

Why Am I Here?

Cameron, have you ever wondered why mankind was created? Why we were put on this earth in the first place? Was it for our benefit? Was mankind created for his own pleasure and comfort? Or were we created for some nobler purpose, perhaps to serve one another? Or to make the world a better place?

To tackle this biggest of big questions, I'll start with our own family. At least I can relate on that level. Besides, I'm sure at some point you'll want to know why you were conceived—the reason for your own existence. And to that question, I do know the answer.

creation was not for your pleasure, your comfort or your benefit. It was not to make you happy or fulfilled. And it was not for you to serve your brothers and sisters—you had none. In fact, your conception had nothing to do with you. Think about it; it couldn't have been about you because you didn't exist yet. In other words, we didn't decide to conceive you as a gesture of good will toward you because, at the time, there was no you!

Mom and I decided to create a child because we wanted to reflect our love for one another in a new creation. Not because we needed a child, but because we wanted one. A little person who shared our DNA, whom we could love and who would love us back.

Basically, it was all about us.

In the same manner, the Bible tells us that man was not created for man, but for God. Not because he needed us, but because he wanted us. After all, God is love, and love is best expressed toward someone else. We are an expression of God's love. In other words, it's not about us at all.

It's about God.

THE BIG LIE

In the Book of Genesis where it all began, God created Adam and Eve and placed them in the Garden of Eden. All kinds of trees grew in the garden—trees pleasing to the eye and good for food. In the middle of the Garden stood the tree of knowledge of good and evil. God commanded Adam that he may eat from any tree in the garden except that one, "for when you eat of it, you will surely die."[14]

Everything seemed to be humming along until the devil slithered into the Garden. "Did God really say, 'You must not eat from any tree in the garden'?" he asked Eve. "You will not surely die." "For God knows that when you eat of it your eyes will be opened, *and you will be like God*, knowing good and evil."[15]

Did you catch it? It's the devil's big lie—we can be like God. It *is* about us. Adam and Eve fell for it in the Garden of Eden, and mankind has been falling for it every since.

Especially me.

---

[14] Genesis 2:17.
[15] Genesis 3:1-5 (emphasis added).

The Self-Made Man

A funny thing happened to me on the way to court one day.

I was hustling along Flagler Street in downtown Miami, barely noticing the other self-absorbed people shuffling by or the merchants mechanically performing their morning rituals. But then it stopped me, almost as if someone screamed out my name. There in a shop window was a little statue of a god-like figure carving himself out of a block of stone. The caption read "Self-Made Man."

Wow, I thought, that could be me. After all, I put myself through college and law school after my parents died. I made it by the sweat of my own brow. No one handed me a thing. I did it my way.

No doubt about it—I was the self-made man.

Unfortunately, I lived that delusion for many years. Of all things, it wasn't until changing your diaper one night that I had a revelation. It started with this question: What are we feeding this kid? Just kidding. It was this: I wonder if you will ever appreciate all the sacrifices we're making for you?

As silly as it sounds to me now, it was only at that moment that it dawned on me—when I was a baby, I didn't change any of my own diapers either. Nor did I get up in the middle of the night to make my bottles or rock myself back to sleep. I didn't teach myself to walk, talk or ride a bike either. My parents graciously endured all of this and more—much more.

I began to think of the tremendous contributions I received from others. Everything from teaching me reading and writing in grade school to torts and contracts in law school. At that moment, it occurred to me that just about everything I know came from someone else . . . from parents, families, friends, coaches and countless teachers and mentors. But most importantly, it came from God, who created it all.

People take pride in saying that they came up the hard way; that they pulled themselves up by their bootstraps. We like to think of ourselves as the masters of our fate and the captains of our souls. But I don't believe it anymore. The self-made man is a lie. We didn't create ourselves.

None of us is self-made.

THE MEANING OF LIFE

The first time I read the Bible cover-to-cover, my naïve goal was to find the one nugget that explained the whole thing. Why was man created? Why are we here? What's the meaning of life? I must admit, it was slow-going through

Leviticus and Numbers, but eventually I came to a passage in the New Testament that I believe lays it out.

One of the most famous and influential men in all of history, and author of much of the New Testament, is the Apostle Paul. In the Book of Acts (which he didn't write), Paul finds himself in Athens. He is dismayed to see that the city is filled with idols honoring the various Greek gods (the ones you studied in seventh grade). Milling about are Greek philosophers who spend their time discussing the latest theories and ideas. Among them are Epicureans, who believe that pleasure is the primary goal in life, and Stoics, who suppress their desire for pleasure, placing thinking above feeling. To this diverse group, Paul shared his belief in the one true God.

Paul's ideas must have been radical even for the Greek philosophers. They invited him to share this "new philosophy" at a council meeting convened near the Acropolis. So Paul, himself a rabbi and a scholar, addressed the council in one of the most memorable speeches in scripture:

> Men of Athens! I see that in every way you are very religious. For as I walked around and looked carefully at your objects of worship, I even found an altar with this inscription:

TO AN UNKNOWN GOD. Now what you worship as unknown I am going to proclaim to you.

The God who made the world and everything in it is the Lord of heaven and earth and does not live in temples built by hands. And he is not served by human hands, as if he needed anything, because he himself gives all men life and breath and everything else. From one man he made every nation of men, that they should inhabit the whole earth; and he determined the times set for them and the exact places where they should live. *God did this so that men would seek him and perhaps reach out for him and find him, though he is not far from each one of us. For in him we live and move and have our being.*[16]

I haven't come across a statement that explains more clearly the reason God created us in the first place. He did it so that we would seek him. Reach out for him. Find him. Love him. Glorify him. In short, he wants a relationship with us.

---

[16] Acts 17:22-28.

Journal

7/3/04

Cameron,

You are a wonderful boy, and I know you will go on to accomplish great things in life. But one thing I hope you'll never say is that you're a self-made man.[17] Nothing could be further from the truth.

Before you were conceived, your mother took fertility medication to assist in your creation. If not for the infertility specialist, you wouldn't have been born. During child birth, you had your umbilical cord wrapped around your neck. If not for the crack team of healthcare professionals at the hospital, you wouldn't have lasted an hour.

In your first months of life, you didn't breastfeed yourself or change any of your own diapers. Later on, you didn't teach yourself how to swing a bat, tennis racquet or golf club. Nor did you teach

---

[17] This journal entry was inspired by a sermon of Rev. Dr. Win Green.

yourself how to tie your shoes, ride a bike or read. Just about everything you've learned came from someone else.

Understand that when I write this, it's as much for my benefit as yours. I always fancied myself as a self-made man. But I've come to realize the fallacy of my reasoning. You see, I didn't change any of my own diapers either. We all need people, lots of them. More importantly, we need God. He made each and everyone one of us, and he made us to depend on him.

My son, the day is coming when you will leave our house. That is a day that I will both dread and relish. I will dread it because you will be independent of Mom and me. A piece of our hearts will walk out the door with you on that day. But we will also relish it because if Mom and I have done our job, you will have become dependent on God. And that's just how it should be.

I love you,

Dad

It's About God

So that's the first lesson, Cameron. Your life really isn't about you. It's about God. You were created to seek him. To reach out for him. To find him. Your life must revolve not around yourself, but around God.

Now that you know you were created for God, you need to know what he expects of you. You're ready to learn the purpose of your life.

LESSON TWO

YOU CAN LIVE WITHOUT ANYTHING, EXCEPT PURPOSE

"THERE ARE TWO GREAT DAYS IN A PERSON'S LIFE—THE DAY WE ARE BORN AND THE DAY WE DISCOVER WHY."

—WILLIAM BARCLAY

DO I MATTER?

On December 16, 1998, Kevin Cole of the United States ejected a 7.5 inch spaghetti strand out of his nostril in a single blow. It was a world record.

Not to be outdone, on May 19, 2001, American Jackie Bibby held eight live rattlesnakes in his mouth by their tails for 12.5 seconds. Another world record.

But here's the topper. On December 5, 2001, Stevie Starr of the United Kingdom swallowed 11 Spanish coins, each with a different date. One-by-one, he then regurgitated each coin on command by date. Yes, that was a world record too.

While reading these bizarre feats of human "achievement" in my worn and cherished volume of Guinness World Records 2003, the question that jumps off the page is not how many or how fast or how extreme. The question is *why?* Why would someone shoot pasta out his nose, stuff live rattle snakes in his mouth or vomit coins?

Why?

The answer seems to be that people want to be the best in the world—at something. It makes little difference what, so long as they're the best. Because if they're the best, then their lives matter. And if their lives matter, then they have meaning.

This principle is true for everyone, not just world record holders. We all need our lives to matter. We need purpose. Without purpose, life is meaningless.

Man's Search for Meaning

Psychiatrist Victor Frankl was a World War II concentration camp survivor whose wife, father, mother and brother all perished at the hands of the Nazis. Frankl wondered why some prisoners were able to endure the unbearable physical and emotional torture of the death camps while others succumbed. He concluded that those who survived had something or someone for which to live. They had purpose. For some, it was religion. For others, it was the hope of one day being reunited with family. For Frankl himself, it was writing his book.

Frankl observed that the survivors had one additional trait—they were able to make sense of their seemingly senseless suffering. His philosophy became known as existentialism, which can be summarized as follows: "To live is to suffer, to survive is to find meaning in the suffering."[18] Frankl was fond of quoting German philosopher Friedrich Nietzsche, who said it this way: "He who has a *why* to live can bear with any *how*."[19]

Unfortunately, the converse also was true in the concentration camps. Even if they were not killed, the prisoners who could not make sense of their suffering still died; they either gave up or committed suicide. When this group of prisoners fully and finally concluded that they no longer had purpose, their lives were over.

---

[18] Victor E. Frankl, *Man's Search for Meaning* (New York: Simon & Schuster, 1984), 9.
[19] Ibid.

I'M A BELIEVER

My father's own experience seems to bear out Frank's point. At 68 years of age, he had seen his share of tragedy—the untimely deaths of his father, brothers, first wife, second wife and even his 14-year-old daughter. He was stricken with bad health too. He had advanced heart disease resulting in open-heart surgery. He was an insulin-dependent diabetic. He had his left leg amputated. He had a pace-maker to regulate his heart.

My dad's health was such a disaster that for the last several years of his life, he was dying. In fact, the only thing that kept him alive to age 68 was his focus on a singular goal.

You see, I'm the youngest child in the family. The baby. When I was 14, my mother died of cancer. Not surprisingly, much of my dad's will to live died with my mother. By that point in his life, his career was long over, many of his friends were gone and his hobbies were basically nonexistent. But he still had a goal—to see me off to college. That was his last purpose in life.

I learned later that when I drove off for college on that fateful day, my dad told my brother Scot that his mission had been completed. His prophesy fulfilled itself. A few weeks later, I got the call at college that dad had died.

You Can Live Without Anything, Except Purpose

A man can live for 40 days without food and three days without water. But without purpose, he doesn't stand a chance.

Is There a Purpose?

While we all need a purpose to survive, the real question is—just what is the purpose? Is it shooting spaghetti out our nose, or is there a grander plan? Is it to be rich, famous and attractive? Or perhaps caring, generous, "good people?" Or is it simply to be happy? Are all purposes created equal?

In a strange way, the question of purpose reminds me of Fred,[20] your Little League coach. Coach Fred was an irascible guy. He knew the game of baseball, but didn't have the patience or the temperament to teach it to a bunch of unruly ten-year-old boys. Always the activist, Mom "volunteered" *me* to serve as assistant coach. I objected that I really didn't know the game well enough to coach it, but she assured me that my real job would be personnel management and public relations. In other words, keep the peace between Coach Fred, the boys and the parents. I assure you, it was no walk in the (ball) park.

---

[20] Some of the names in this book have been changed to protect the not so innocent.

There was one practice that drives home the purpose principle for me. Coach Fred was running a bunting drill. As you know, a bunt is where the batter doesn't swing, but simply holds his bat in the hitting zone and allows the ball to make contact with it. The idea is to deaden the hit so the base-runners can advance or the batter can get to first base while the opposing fielders run in to make the play. Ideally, the ball should end up about midway between the catcher and the pitcher down either the first-base or third-base line.

Anyway, the boys weren't executing the bunting drill, and Coach Fred was worked up to the point where his face was beet red and the veins were bulging from his neck. Sensing disaster, I stepped in and offered to finish the drill. Coach Fred readily accepted.

I had you boys drop your bats and line up single-file behind home plate. I then asked if you knew what a perfect bunt looked like. You all assured me you did. One-by-one, I had you and your teammates take a baseball and *place* it in the field where you thought it should come to rest with a perfect bunt. The first boy placed his ball right in front of home plate. Wrong. The second boy placed it a few inches from the first. Wrong as well. Boy after boy, they were wrong, wrong, wrong.

Most of the boys placed the ball within a five-foot radius of home plate—they were all wrong.

The coach had been screaming at you boys for failing to reach a goal that had never been explained. The team had no idea what a successful bunt looked like. No idea that laying down a bunt wasn't just getting in the way of the ball and letting it land wherever it might.

As it turns out, Cameron, bunting is a lot like life—whether we know it or not, both have a very definite purpose.

God's Purpose for Our Lives

2,000 years ago, a man walked the earth saying he was God incarnate. Imagine that—God in the flesh. Now if I said I was God, you'd call me a liar. And you'd be right. You could easily prove that I'm not God. But when Jesus Christ said he was God, no one could prove him wrong. He performed amazing miracles. He healed cripples. He made blind men see. He walked on water and raised the dead. Hundreds of people saw him die on the cross, only to see him walking around again three days later. And to this day, no one has found his corpse. That's because it doesn't exist. Jesus ascended to heaven, where he lives today.

When Jesus was on earth, he said amazing things. These things were faithfully recorded in a book—the Bible. Sure, there are other books about life. But there's only one book with the words of the one who created life. Surely, a book like that is worth studying.

God has a clear and unmistakable purpose for our lives, and it's recorded in the Bible. Here's how Jesus explained it:

> Love the Lord your God with all your heart and with all your soul and with all your mind. This is the first and greatest commandment. And the second is like it: Love your neighbor as yourself. All the Law and the Prophets hang on these two commandments.[21]

With this explanation, Jesus summed up the entire Old Testament. Our first purpose is to love God. That's why we were made in the first place. Our second purpose it to love others. Love God, love others. This is called the "Great Commandment."

But that's not all. Before Jesus ascended into heaven, he commissioned his disciples as follows:

> All authority in heaven and on earth has been given to me. Therefore, go and make disciples of all nations, baptizing them in the name of the Father and of the Son and of the Holy

---

[21] Matthew 22:37.

> Spirit, and teaching them to obey everything I have commanded you. And surely I am with you always, to the very end of the age.[22]

This directive, known as the "Great Commission," applies not just to Jesus' disciples or to clergy or to people in full-time ministry; it applies to all of us. We are to tell others about Jesus Christ. It is not a suggestion; it is a requirement.

Distilled to its essence, this is our purpose on earth according to God's word:

1. **Love God.** This is the first and greatest commandment.

2. **Love others.** The way we show love for others is primarily by serving them.

3. **Share Christ.** "Go and make disciples of all nations" is our commission to be evangelists, sharing the gospel with all nonbelievers. Of course, this assumes that we first believe in Christ ourselves.

The beauty of these three purposes is that we're never too old to fulfill them. And no matter how long we live, we still have more to do. Jesus Christ modeled this even at the end of his life. While he hung dying on the cross, he

---

[22] Matthew 28:17-20.

said, "Father, forgive them, for they know not what they do."[23] *He loved others.* He then forgave the sins of the criminal who hung on the cross next to him—*he made a disciple.*[24] And with his final breath, Jesus said, "Father, into your hands I commit my spirit."[25] *He loved God his father supremely.* From his birth in a manger to his death on the cross, Jesus' entire life revolved around these three purposes.

Not only are the three life purposes relevant as long as we draw breath, they extend into eternity. Our good works in this life may not change the fact that we're going to heaven, but they will impact our experience in heaven. More importantly, whether we share Christ with others will determine where *they* spend eternity. In other words, all three purposes have eternal significance. They transcend time, space and, most importantly, ourselves.

A Purpose Worth Living For

If we accept our mission—to love God supremely, to love others, and to share Christ—our lives will not be our own. And they will not be over when our kids go off to college, when we retire, when we're sick, when we're suffering or facing tragedy, or even when we're dying.

---

[23] Luke 23:34.
[24] Luke 22:40-43.
[25] Luke 22:46.

Even as we approach the end of our life, there's always our God to honor, love to give, and Christ to imitate and share.

In the first lesson, I introduced you to the Apostle Paul, one of the most famous and influential men who ever lived. Unlike Christ, Paul was just a flawed man, so we can relate to him on a different level. In fact, he was a Jew like me. Before becoming Paul, he was Saul the Tent Maker. Amazingly, his early life was devoted to persecuting Christians. Then one day Saul met Jesus Christ, and everything changed. He became a new creation, with a new name, a new spirit and a new mission: to love God, to love others, and to share Christ. Paul went on to become a great man. Not because his flaws disappeared—they didn't—but because he had a new, Godly purpose—and he fulfilled it.

First and foremost, Paul loved God. He placed God above all else and let nothing get in the way of their relationship. He worshipped him, honored him, trusted him, obeyed him, thanked him, praised him, surrendered to him, served him, studied his word and glorified him. And he did all this despite imprisonment and persecution—and ultimately execution. Paul loved God supremely.

Paul also loved others. In his often quoted letter to the church in Corinth, Paul wrote this about love: "If I have the gift of prophecy and can fathom all mysteries and all knowledge, and if I have a faith that can move mountains, but have not love, I am nothing."[26] Paul understood that the best way to demonstrate love for others is by serving them.

But what really sets Paul apart is that he is the greatest evangelist the world has ever known. He traveled the earth, endured seemingly impossible circumstances, and preached the gospel of Jesus Christ with a knowledge, spirit and conviction that has never been surpassed. He shared Christ like no other.

At the end of Paul's life, when he was facing death by execution, he spoke these final words to his protégé Timothy: "I have fought the good fight, I have finished the race, I have kept the faith."[27] In other words, he left it all on the field. He gave everything he had. And he did it for a worthy cause. He had purpose until the very end.

I want those to be my last words too. I don't want my mission to be accomplished until I draw my last breath. I don't want to live for myself; I want to live for something bigger. For something noble. And I don't want to die without a fight—not a fight for me but a fight that's worth fighting. I want to fight for God and for others. I want to die with my boots on, fighting a good and noble fight.

---

[26] 1 Corinthians 13:2.
[27] 2 Timothy 4:7.

So I have just one question, Cameron—are you with me? Are you willing to accept your mission to love God, love others and share Christ? If you are, get ready for a fight.

LESSON THREE

LIFE IS HARD—CHOOSE TO FIGHT

"IT IS NOT THE CRITIC WHO COUNTS; NOT THE MAN WHO POINTS OUT HOW THE STRONG MAN STUMBLED, OR WHERE THE DOER OF DEEDS COULD HAVE DONE THEM BETTER. THE CREDIT BELONGS TO THE MAN WHO IS ACTUALLY IN THE ARENA, WHOSE FACE IS MARRED BY DUST AND SWEAT AND BLOOD; WHO STRIVES VALIANTLY; WHO ERRS AND COMES UP SHORT AGAIN AND AGAIN; WHO KNOWS THE GREAT ENTHUSIASMS, THE GREAT DEVOTIONS; WHO SPENDS HIMSELF IN A WORTHY CAUSE, WHO AT BEST, KNOWS IN THE END THE TRIUMPH OF HIGH ACHIEVEMENT, AND WHO, AT THE WORST, IF HE FAILS, AT LEAST FAILS WHILE DARING GREATLY, SO THAT HIS PLACE SHALL NEVER BE WITH THOSE COLD AND TIMID SOULS WHO KNOW NEITHER VICTORY NOR DEFEAT."[28]

—THEODORE ROOSEVELT

---

[28] Theodore Roosevelt, "Citizenship in a Republic," speech at the Sorbonne, Paris, April 23, 1910.

Gonna Fly Now

I make no apologies for it. *Rocky* is my favorite movie and, in my view, the best movie ever made (I make no comment on *Rocky II* through *VI*).[29] I know, I know. People say *Gone with the Wind* and *Citizen Kane* are better choices. But let's face it, those films contain no boxing.

Set in 1976, *Rocky* is the story of a big-hearted, journeyman fighter. Life seems to have passed by Rocky. He's been relegated to collecting debts for a loan shark and fighting against guys with names like Spider Rico. Even by his own estimation, Rocky is a loser, a has-been, a nobody.

Rocky's luck takes a dramatic turn when he gets a million-to-one shot at the title against the undefeated heavyweight champion of the world, Apollo Creed. So Rocky begins to train. He starts slowly, cramping up on his first run, but he gradually improves. He drinks raw eggs. He does road work. He hits the weights and does one-handed push-ups. He pounds raw meat. He spars. And in the climactic training scene, Rocky sprints up the steps of the Philadelphia Museum of Art. At the top, he turns, looks out over the city and raises his hands in anticipatory victory, the theme song *Gonna Fly Now* reaching its crescendo.

---

[29] *Rocky*, written by Sylvester Stallone, directed by John G. Alvidsen (MGM: 1976)

Yes, Rocky is going to beat the champ!

Then reality sets in. It's the night before the big fight. Rocky can't sleep, so he wanders into the auditorium. Standing in the center of the ring, he looks up in awe at the banner hanging from the rafters with the larger-than-life image of the champ. He doesn't see a man, he sees a god. An unbeatable giant. Then his eyes scan across the cavernous arena until they settle on his own banner. All he can see is the imperfection—the artist painted the wrong color on his boxing trunks. Rocky's shoulders slump, his head hangs. He leaves the arena, beaten before the first punch is thrown.

Have you been there before, son? I have, many times.

Dejected, Rocky goes home to his girlfriend Adrian. Sitting on the edge of the bed, he mutters, "I can't beat him." Adrian awakens and asks what he's talking about. "Who am I kidding?" Rocky says. "He's the champ, and I'm a nobody." Adrian protests, but Rocky knows better. "I was thinkin'," he continues. "It don't really matter anyway. I don't care if I lose. I don't care if Apollo opens up my head. I just wanna go the distance. No one has ever gone the distance with Apollo. If I'm still standing after 15 rounds, then I'll know for the first time in my life that I weren't just another bum from the neighborhood."

In that glorious moment, Rocky's mission changes. It's no longer about winning; it's about going the distance. It's about being able to stand up to a giant. It's about fighting the good fight.

Of course, Rocky does go the distance, and he almost wins the fight to boot. That's not the point of the story though. I love how the announcer's voice trails off in the background when he reads the split decision. It's an afterthought. Sure, it's relevant to Apollo Creed, who raises his hands in victory. But Apollo knows he almost lost his title to a nobody. As for Rocky, well, he went the distance with the heavyweight champion of the world!

Facing Your Giant

The Rocky movie makes two important points. The first is obvious—life is not about winning or losing; it's about engaging the fight. It's about facing our giants and going the distance. The second point is more subtle. You see, the giant Rocky was fighting was not so much Apollo Creed, but the demons in his own mind— the feelings of self-doubt, insignificance, and inadequacy. Apollo Creed was Rocky's foil, but lack of self-esteem was his giant.

As it turns out, we all have a giant—all of us. Like Rocky, it may be insecurity and self-doubt. Or it might be greed, materialism, lust, anger, jealousy, fear, worry, addiction, depression, regret or lack of self-control. Some are haunted by their past. Others feel all alone. Some believe they're too old or too young. The giant might be a troubled relationship, lack of money or poor health. For some, it's a dead-end job. For others, it's having no job at all. And for many, the giant is not having a compelling vision for life.

But we all have a giant—that one obstacle that towers above our other problems and has the capacity to thwart all forward progress. So I ask you, son, what's your giant?

Some of us go through life thinking we have no defects, no giant at all. For those people, I have a diagnosis. I know because I'm one of them. Our giant is pride.

A few years ago, our dear friends Win and Stephanie Green were moving, and we were helping them pack. Stephanie was giving some mementos away to her friends, and she gave Mom some handmade jewelry. "I have something for you too, Spencer," she said. Stephanie disappeared into her library and emerged with a little paperback entitled "Humility." At the time, I thought it was just a random selection of a book otherwise destined for the trash heap. I didn't think much about the book until six months later when I noticed it on the shelf. It finally dawned on me that Stephanie thought I could benefit by reading it—that my arrogance, lack of humility and pride might go well with a slice of humble pie. I ran to tell Kat my discovery, but somehow, she seemed to know already. I swallowed hard and asked, "Does anyone else feel this way about me?" She just smiled and looked away.

You see, that's the way it is with pride. You have a nine-foot-tall giant towering over you, but you can't see him. He's obvious to everyone—except you.

And then there's the rest of the population. Those who are battling so many giants, they can't limit it to just one. My suggestion to those folks is that if they really reflect on it, there's that one giant who stands about a head taller than the rest. There's one giant who seems to be leading the battalion of giants. My advice to them? Focus on the lead giant.

One more thing. Throughout the seasons of our lives, we have different giants. The truth is that life is hard. And it's hard for everyone—even the ones who seem to have it easy.

As long as I'm being brutally honest, not much of my life has been easy. When my family moved from New York to Miami when I was seven, I cried every day for a month. Second grade at a new school was hard, and third grade didn't get any easier. My mother died when I was in eighth grade; that was really hard. In fact, all of school was hard, right through law school. Being a teenager was hard. Having my father die when I was a college freshman was hard. The following year, my girlfriend Kat (your mother) had brain surgery just a few months after we met. It was hard. In my twenties, learning how to be a lawyer and a husband at the same time was hard. In my thirties, starting my own law firm while becoming a new dad was hard.

Now in my forties, experiencing the onset of my body's physical deterioration (punctuated by several orthopedic surgeries) has been hard. Work is hard. Commuting an hour each way to and from the office is hard. Going to the gym every day is hard. Eating healthy is hard. Writing this book is hard. Being a Christian in a fallen world is hard.

Don't get me wrong. I'm not saying that life isn't wonderful. It is. But let's face it, it's hard. And it's filled with giants. So I ask you, what do you do with all these hardships? How do you survive in the land of the giants? To answer these questions, I need to go back even earlier than 1976. I need to go back 3,000 years—to the original Rocky.

The Original Rocky

A long, long time ago, God used prophets to anoint the kings of Israel. The very first king-maker was the Prophet Samuel. At God's direction, Samuel anointed Saul as the first King of Israel.

King Saul stared off strong, but later disobeyed God. Unbeknownst to Saul, God directed Samuel to anoint a new king, one of the sons of a man named Jesse. So Saul traveled to Jesse's home and spotted his eldest son, Eliab. Eliab must have been quite a physical specimen. Samuel thought to himself, "Surely the Lord's anointed stands before the Lord. But the Lord said to Samuel, 'Do not consider his appearance or his height, for I have rejected him. The Lord does not look at the things man looks at. Man looks at the outward appearance, but the Lord looks at the *heart*.'"[30]

So Jesse paraded the rest of his boys before Samuel—seven of them—but none was chosen. "Are these all the sons you have?" Samuel inquired. "There is still the youngest, but he is tending the sheep" Jesse replied. Samuel had Jesse send for his youngest boy, David. "Rise and anoint him," the Lord said. "He is the one."[31]

What? Rise and anoint him? What was it about young David that was different than his seven brothers? The text doesn't say exactly, but it does give us a clue. It says the Lord looks at the heart—a recurring theme throughout the Bible. The only thing I can conclude is that David's heart somehow was different from his brothers'. The nature of the difference becomes clear later in the story.

---

[30] 1 Samuel 16:6-7 (emphasis added).
[31] 1 Samuel 16:10-12.

King Saul, unaware that David was his replacement, took a shine to the young man. He noticed that David was handsome, that he played the harp and had a reputation for bravery. So impressed was Saul with the young man that he made David his armor bearer.

At this time, Israel was at war with the Philistines, which had a champion, a nine-foot-tall giant named Goliath. For forty days, Goliath stood at the battle line and taunted Israel:

> "Why do you come out and line up for battle? Am I not a Philistine, and are you not the servants of Saul? Choose a man and have him come down to me. If he is able to fight and kill me, we will become your subjects; but if I overcome him and kill him, you will become our subjects and serve us." Then the Philistine said, "This day I defy the ranks of Israel! Give me a man and let us fight each other." On hearing the Philistine's words, Saul and all the Israelites were dismayed and terrified.[32]

Among the terrified Israeli warriors were David's three older brothers, including Eliab. David, on the other hand, was too young for battle, so he helped by bringing provisions to the soldiers. In

---

[32] 1 Samuel 17:4-11.

other words, he was the water-boy. But when David heard the obscenities the giant was spewing, his blood began to boil.

His brothers told him to mind his own business, but David couldn't. He went straight to King Saul and volunteered to fight the giant himself! Saul, of course, thought David crazy. He reminded David that he was just a boy, and Goliath, well, he was a giant. But David pestered Saul until he relented. With a bit of foreshadowing, Saul dressed the future king in his own armor. But David had never worn armor. After clunking around the royal palace a bit, he removed it , took up his wooden staff and gathered five smooth stones from the stream.

With sling in hand, David approached his giant—his Apollo Creed.

Goliath moved in for the kill, but was surprised to see that David was "only a boy, ruddy and handsome." Goliath mocked and cursed David, saying that he would serve his flesh to the animals. David was not intimidated. Like Babe Ruth pointing to left field, he replied, "You come against me with sword and spear and javelin, but I come against you in the name of the Lord Almighty . . . Today I will strike you down and cut off your head . . . and the whole world will know that there is a God in Israel."[33]

---

[33] 1 Samuel 17:45-46.

With that, David loaded one of the stones in his sling, fired it at the giant and hit him right between the eyes. Goliath fell to the ground, dead! For dramatic effect, David stood over Goliath, removed the giant's sword from its scabbard and cut off his head. Fear stricken, the Philistine army retreated in horror. But the Israeli warriors now had courage. They gave chase and routed the enemy.

I guess Andrew Jackson was right when he said, "One man with courage makes a majority."[34] Especially if he's fighting with God at his side.

A Man After God's Own Heart

Of course, you already knew the story of David and Goliath. Everyone does. People have been telling it for 3,000 years, and they'll be telling it for another 3,000.

And that King David, what a guy—warrior, musician, lyricist (he wrote most of the Psalms). Did you know he was also a dancer? When David brought the ark containing the Ten Commandments back to the Holy City of Jerusalem, he donned a linen priest's apron and danced before the Lord with all his might. His wife Michal observed the scene from her window. There was her husband, dancing and leaping, and in front of the slave girls no less! When David finally came home that evening,

---

[34] Andrew Jackson.

she lit into him: "How the king of Israel has distinguished himself this evening, disrobing in the sight of the slave girls of his servants like any vulgar fellow would!"[35] But David was indignant: "It was before the Lord" I was dancing, not the slave girls. And undignified? Stay tuned, he told Michal, "I will become even more undignified than this!"[36]

Incidentally, this story is why I never judge the way people worship God. Scripture tells us that Michal died childless.

Now I want to be clear, David was no saint. He committed both adultery and murder! Yet, amazingly, he is the only human being in the Bible described as "a man after God's own heart."[37] Another reference to the heart. Which leads me back to the question, what was it about David's heart that was so special? How was his heart like God's? And where can I get one?

As I reflect on it, I think it comes down to this. Dave had unshakable faith. And, unlike his brothers, he volunteered to fight! He was passionate too. Yeah, that David was a giant-slaying, harp-playing, song-writing, God-loving fool. And he danced. Boy, did he dance. When it was time to fight, he fought. But when it was time to dance, he danced.

---

[35] 2 Samuel 6:20.
[36] 2 Samuel 6:21:22.
[37] Acts 13:22.

If I had to express the heart formula as an equation, it would look like this:

Faith + Action + Passion = HEART

The Dream Sequence

Every so often, I have this dream. I'm sitting on the couch staring at a nine-foot-tall giant. And I'm having a case of the pity-me's. There I am, stuck on the couch, paralyzed with fear and self-pity. I stare at the giant and wonder to myself: "Wow, how did he get so big? And why is he picking on *me*? What did I do to him? Why did he take my parents? Where was God then? Why didn't he deliver me? Why is life so hard? And why am I still gripped with sin—with pride and greed? When will I catch a break? When will God show up and fight my giants? When will he get me off this couch?"

Now here's the part where it gets really weird (as if the giant isn't weird enough). Just when I'm about to give up, an angel appears right in my living room. Turns out, it's King David! But he's not a boy anymore. He's older, with gray hair and a flowing beard. Sort of like the Ghost of Hanukah Past. He says he's been watching me from heaven, pacing the sidelines, waiting for me to act. Just like he did 3,000 years ago when he watched as the Israelites were paralyzed with fear by the giant Goliath. He says he just couldn't take it anymore, so he came down from heaven for a little half-time pep talk. How ironic, I think to myself. At 45, I'm in the half-time of my life.

So King David walks over to me, takes a knee and gets right in my face.

"Spence, do you know what time it is?"

"I . . . I . . . I don't know," I stammer, still in shock from the vision. "Around midnight?"

"No, it's time to man up! You don't need pity. What you need is a backbone! Where's your heart?! Did you forget that you are God's mighty warrior?! Did you forget that he can make you more than a conqueror?!"

With that, David rises to his feet and says, "Spence, it's time to join the battle. Because it's in the battle that God builds your character. It's in the battle that God shapes your heart. It's in the battle that God explodes your faith. It's never on the couch. It's never in the rocking chair. It's never on the sidelines. It's in the battle where you meet God, where you come face to face with Jesus Christ."

"But there's a catch," David reveals. "The battle is the Lord's, but you must take the first step. He will not levitate you off that couch. It's always been that way—always. When the Israelites stood ready to cross the Jordan River to enter the Promised Land, God did not part the water until the priests got their feet wet. Nor did God intercede for Abraham until he was ready to plunge the knife into his son Isaac. And Peter didn't walk on water until he got out of the boat. God will fight with you, but he will not fight for you."

"And one more thing," David says. "That story about Goliath and me. I must admit, I like that one myself. But if you keep reading through First and Second Samuel, you'll see there were other battles with other giants. Sometimes I got the best of them, and sometimes they got the best me. I always kept fighting though, no matter what."

"So there's just one thing you need to do," David says. And then he leans over and whispers in my ear that one word that shakes me down to my soul.

"Fight" he says. "Get off the couch and FIGHT!"

Then David starts to fade away. "I have to go back to heaven now," he says. "I'm working on a new dance."

And with that, he's gone. It's just me again—alone with the giant. But then I hear another voice.

This time it's God.

"My son, are you willing to join the battle? Are you ready to fight?"

"God, I'm a proud man," I say. "Teach me humility, and then I can get off this couch."

God replies, "I know all about it. What you need to do, my son, is serve the needy. Make yourself low and wash their feet."

"But God," I say, "I don't think you heard me. I need you to make me humble before I can do that."

"I heard you perfectly," God answers. "Wash their feet, and I'll teach you everything there is to know about humility."

"And what about my greed?" I ask.

"That's simple," God replies. "Just write a check."

"I think you have it backwards, God. You need to make me generous first."

"No, I think you have it backwards," God responds. "Write a check, and you'll become generous."

"But I've had a hard life, God. I'm weary and I'm scared. Can't you just make things easy for me?"

"Sure I can," he says. "But I won't. Because then you'd think you succeeded on your own merit. Your character would never develop. Your faith would never grow. And your heart would never change. But if you take the first step, I promise I'll be with you. I will make you more than a conqueror."

So I rise up off the couch, and take a step. "Wow, that wasn't so hard."

"Good," God says. "Now take another."

So I do. And pretty soon, I'm high-stepping all over my living room. That is, until I remember that the giant is still there.

"You can do it," God assures me.

I swallow hard and take a step toward my giant. And then another. And another. Until I'm right in front of him, staring up into the face shield of his helmet. I lift my trembling hand and knock on his armored chest. But there's no answer. I knock again. "Hello, Mr. Giant." Still no answer. So I lift up his face shield, and to my great surprise, there's nothing inside. My giant is hollow!

I can't believe it. I spent all that time worrying about a giant, and he existed only in my mind.

Then I wake up.

The Impossible Dream

Son, don't expect life to be easy—because it's not. It's hard. But that's the best part. All the great things in life are hard. If they weren't, they wouldn't be great. If everyone could hit a baseball like A-Rod, throw a pass like Peyton Manning or swing a golf club like Tiger Woods, those guys wouldn't be superstars. If everyone could ride a bike like Lance Armstrong or swim like Michael Phelps, no one would marvel at their accomplishments. Their feats are amazing because they're hard. Don't ever look for the easy way; it's the hard way that makes the man.

Not only that, it's the pain and suffering that give context for all joy in life. Without suffering, joy has no meaning. Before the Israelites entered the Land of Milk and Honey, they wondered in the desert for 40 years. And before Resurrection Sunday, there was Crucifixion Friday. There are no shortcuts. To get to heaven, you have to go through hell.

And please, don't get too hung up on results. Remember, it's the impossible fights that fire our imagination. Rocky fought a giant and lost. In the classic story, *To Kill a Mockingbird*, small-town lawyer Atticus Finch defended an innocent black man accused of raping a white woman—and lost. And Don Quixote tilted at windmills. He didn't win. But those characters are heroes, not because they won—they didn't—but because they fought. They are champions because they marched into hell for a heavenly cause.

As a civil defense lawyer, I can relate to those stories. My profession is hard. If I were a plaintiff's lawyer, I would get better, more winnable cases as I progressed in my career. The cases with clear liability and huge damages. For us defense lawyers, it's exactly the opposite. We're defending those huge cases brought by the best plaintiff's lawyers. The more experience we get, the harder and scarier our job becomes. In fact, I know from the start that many of my cases can't be won. I recently lost a trial to the tune of $38 million! Sure, every once in a while I may snatch victory from the jaws of defeat. But if I focused on the outcome, it would get pretty depressing. I choose instead to focus on the fight—to answer the call to battle, to fight the good fight, to go the distance.

Recall the Apostle Paul's final words to his protégé Timothy: "I have fought the good fight, I have finished the race, I have kept the faith."[38] Notice what he doesn't say. He doesn't say he won the fight or the race. It was enough that he fought the fight and finished the race—and kept his faith in the process. That should be enough for you too. On your death bed, you may regret the battles you lost, but you'll never forgive yourself for the ones you didn't fight.

In the hit Broadway musical *Man of La Mancha*,[39] the Don Quixote character described

---

[38] 2 Timothy 4:7.
[39] *Man of La Mancha*, music by Mitch Leigh, lyrics by Joe Dorion (Broadway 1965). This was my mother's and Kat's father's favorite song. We adopted it as our wedding song and life song.

the mission of a knight in similar terms—as an *Impossible Dream*:

> It is the mission of each true knight... His duty... nay, his privilege! To dream the impossible dream, To fight the unbeatable foe, To bear with unbearable sorrow To run where the brave dare not go; To right the unrightable wrong.
>
> To love pure and chaste from afar, To try, when your arms are too weary, To reach the unreachable star!
>
> This is my Quest to follow that star, No matter how hopeless, no matter how far, To fight for the right Without question or pause, To be willing to march into hell For a heavenly cause!
>
> And I know, if I'll only be true To this glorious Quest, That my heart will lie peaceful and calm When I'm laid to my rest.
>
> And the world will be better for this, That one man, scorned and covered with scars, Still strove, with his last ounce of courage, To reach the unreachable star!

Like the song says, Cameron, you have a mission. A noble mission. But you are also free to reject it. It's your choice. It's the same choice that confronted fictional characters Rocky, Atticus Finch and Don Quixote. The same choice posed to historical figures King David, the Apostle Paul and even Jesus Christ. The same choice facing every man since the beginning of time.

The choice is this: You can take the easy way out. You can spend your life wondering why it's so hard; why bad things happen to good people. Or you can be an agent of change. You can choose to fight for what is right; for what is good and noble. If you fight—if you just take the first step—I promise, God will be with you. Remember, it's in the battlefield of life where you meet God. He will make you more than a conqueror.[40]

Cameron, you will have hardship in this life. When you do, I hope you choose to fight.

And when the fighting is over, I hope you dance.

Now, if you're going to fight, you'll need a code of conduct for the battle.

---

[40] Romans 8:37.

Lesson Four

Character is What You Do When No One is Looking

"Men of genius are admired. Men of power, feared. But only men of character are trusted."

—Arthur Friedman

"God is more concerned about your character than your comfort."

—Anonymous

Ping Golf Clubs—Part I

As a new lawyer, it seemed like a good time for me to get back into golf. A visit to the local golf discounter was in order. After a quick look around the shop, I struck pay dirt—a slightly used set of Ping irons in mint condition. The only problem was I didn't have much money at the time, and the price was a bit steep. And as I soon learned, the hard-boiled golf shop owner wasn't in much of a mood to negotiate.

"Hi there," I greeted the proprietor. "I'm interested in the used set of Ping irons over there. Do you think you could do a little better on the price?"

"They're already discounted," he said gruffly. "What did you say your name was?"

"Spencer," I answered.

"Spencer what?" he asked.

"Spencer Silverglate," I replied.

"What kind of a name is Silverglate?" he shot back.

"Uhh . . . I don't know. American, I guess."

"Hmmh," he grunted. "What do you do for a living?"

"I'm a lawyer".

"Oh, I have a million lawyer jokes. What do you call 30 lawyers at the bottom of the ocean? A good start!"

"Good one. Hey, do you think you could knock 50 bucks off the clubs?"

"I told you, they're already discounted. Plus, you're a rich lawyer. You can afford it."

"Actually, I'm just starting out. Would you consider throwing in that Ping golf bag."

"Nope. That's one of my best-sellers."

It was time to play my last card. "I'll be back in a minute," I told him.

I went to my car to retrieve my old set of clubs. "How about a trade-in on these?" I asked.

"Are you kidding me?" he shot back. "Did you get those for your bar mitzvah?"

Wow, that was a bit anti-Semitic, I thought to myself (actually, I did get them for my bar mitzvah, but still, that was a low blow). This guy was really getting under my skin. Every cell in my body wanted to tell him off. But oh, those Pings.

I ultimately left the store with the new clubs—and the bag—a bit less pride and a lot less money. There I was, a budding litigator, badly beaten in a negotiation with a purveyor of used golf clubs.

When I got home, I told Kat all about the experience. Then I took a look at the receipt. And then another look. I couldn't believe my eyes. After all that, the guy forgot to charge me for the golf bag.

Sweet victory!

"Aren't you going to call him?" Kat asked. "Call him?!" I shouted. "Are you kidding me? This guy was a jerk. He took advantage of me. And he got just what he deserved. Plus, he'll never know."

"Whatever you think," she replied.

I hate it when she does that. Besides, I was right, and he was wrong. I was justified. Wasn't I?

What the World Says

So here's the question. By what code of conduct should we live our lives? What do we do in the gap between legality and morality—with conduct that isn't exactly illegal, but wrong nonetheless? And whose version of morality governs?

As kids, we're taught the Golden Rule, "Do unto others as you would have them do unto you." As adults, the rule turns into, "Treat others the way they treat you." I can't tell you how many lawyers I've heard say they start off every case being nice—until the opposing counsel gives them a reason not to be. Then they give it right back. Their morals are dictated by the other guy's behavior. If he's a gentleman, I'll be a gentleman. If he's a jerk, I'll be a jerk. What kind of credo is that?

Some people justify their vengeance with the Old Testament adage, "An eye for an eye and a tooth for a tooth." Never mind that the verse is directed to the government—not individuals—to mete out fair punishment for crimes. What authority gives individuals the right to administer punishment for perceived wrongs against themselves? The answer is the world's authority.

Donald Trump says, "When someone screws you, screw them back 15 times over."[41] Of course, The Donald didn't invent revenge; it's been around since recorded time. The Roman author Phaedrus wrote, "All the old knives that have rusted in my back, I thrust in yours."[42] Homer wrote in the Iliad that revenge "is sweeter far than flowing honey."[43] Shakespeare's Shylock said, "If it will feed nothing else, it will feed my revenge."[44]

Yes, revenge has been around for a while. And it's alive and well today. Just Google the word "revenge" on the Internet and see how many hits you get. RevengeGuy.com, RevengeLady.com, GetRevengeOnYourEx.com, RevengeUnlimited.com. The list goes on for several pages.

The world tells us to give the other guy a taste of his own medicine. And if no one's watching, even better. Plus, it's okay to fudge a little. After all, everyone cheats on their taxes, right? If the sales clerk hands you too much change, her employer can afford it. The hotel won't miss

---

[41] The San Diego Union Tribune, December 4, 2005.
[42] Fables—Appendix (VI, 11).
[43] Homer, The Iliad (XVIII, 109).
[44] William Shakespeare, *The Merchant of Venice* (Shylock at III, i).

a few towels. It doesn't matter what you view on the Internet; no one's getting hurt. Drinking and driving isn't a crime unless you get caught. And what your wife doesn't know won't hurt her. Besides, what happens in Vegas, stays in Vegas.

Our own family's experiences with bad behavior in Little League could be a reality show. Mom was the team scorekeeper. During a playoff game, Mom realized the other team's scorer recorded one too many runs—for us. Mom reported it to your coach, who decided not to say anything. His reasoning—the other team would never find out.

In another game, the opposing coach played his ace pitcher—a 12-year-old—without any rest from the prior night's game. The justification—they needed a win. Can you imagine? Winning a Little League game was more important than a boy's health.

And then there was the game where our hitters were being heckled mercilessly—by an opposing player's *mother*! As if her verbal taunts weren't bad enough, she hung "K's" on the fence every time one of our batters struck out. What lesson was she teaching the kids?

The world tells us that winning is more important than how you play the game. Like the woman who wanted so badly for her daughter to win the essay contest for Hannah Montana tickets. She wrote that the little girl's father was killed in combat in Iraq. It turns out that the father, who had never even served in the military, was alive and well stateside. At what price victory?

The latest scandal on the financial pages involves Bernie Madoff, a New York money manager who committed fraud to the tune of $50 Billion. That's "illion" with a "B." His clients included not just wealthy folk, but colleges and charitable institutions as well.

Our politicians are no better than our business leaders. New York's former attorney general Elliot Spitzer is doing time for soliciting prostitutes. Illinois Mayor Rod Blagoyavich is being investigated for attempting to sell an Illinois senate seat. President Clinton told the American public, "I did not have sex with that woman."

To whom then can we turn for a code of conduct?

What about sports stars? Tiger Woods cheated on his wife. Repeatedly. Homerun king Barry Bonds is widely believed to have cheated with steroids. Ditto Roger Clemens and Alex Rodriguez. Track star Marion Jones was convicted of using performance enhancing drugs in the Olympics. How about the NFL? O.J. Simpson is now serving up to 20 years for armed robbery—a light sentence for those who think he got away with murder. As of this writing, Atlanta Falcons quarterback Michael Vick is in jail for running an illegal dog-fighting operation. College players aren't immune either. A University of Florida football player was just thrown off the team for stealing a laptop.

And what about celebrities? You can count on one hand the ones who've been married to the same person for more than five years. Many live a life of excess and self-indulgence. Consider the example set by Madonna, Brittany Spears, Lindsey Lohan and Mariah Carey, to name a few. If you want to know how to behave, you probably shouldn't look to celebrities.

Even church leaders aren't immune. Just look at Pastors Jimmy Swaggert and Jim Baker.

In a recent survey of 725 teens ages 13 to 18, 40% said that lying, cheating and violence are necessary to succeed. Where would they get such a notion? They've been taking cues from celebrities, politicians, professional athletes, business people and religious leaders.[45]

I could go on, but you get the point. We desperately need a code of conduct by which to live, but the world doesn't seem to supply one. Where then can we turn for guidance?

The answer is simple—Joseph.

---

[45] Eric Conroy, "Violence OK, Say 40% of Teens," Miami Herald, January 14, 2008.

GOD IS WATCHING

Abraham, Isaac and Jacob are the patriarchs of Judaism. Jacob, also called Israel, had twelve sons (the twelve tribes of Israel). His favorite was Joseph. Unfortunately, his brothers knew it, and they hated Joseph for it. It didn't help matters that Joseph told everyone about his dreams—the ones where his brothers bowed down to him. In a fit of jealous rage, the brothers sold Joseph into slavery.

Joseph ended up in Egypt as a servant for a guy named Potiphar, the captain of Pharaoh's guard. But Joseph had God's favor, and he prospered in everything he did. Potiphar was so impressed with the young man that he put him in charge of all his affairs. Not only was Joseph successful, he was handsome too. It didn't take long for Potiphar's wife to notice Joseph, and soon she began to seduce him.

Every day Potiphar's wife propositioned Joseph. Everyday he rejected her advances: "My master has withheld nothing from me except you, because you are his wife. How then could I do such a wicked thing and sin against *God*?"[46]

Did you catch it? Joseph was concerned for his master's welfare, but he was more concerned about sinning against God.

---

[46] Genesis 39:9 (emphasis added).

The situation came to a head one day when Joseph was alone in the house with Potiphar's wife. She caught Joseph by his cloak and said "come to bed with me!" Joesph's master wasn't home, and no one was watching. He may have been tempted to sin, but instead, "he left his cloak in her hand and ran out of the house."[47] He did the right thing—even though it cost him. He was thrown in jail when Potiphar's wife lied to her husband that Joseph had tried to take advantage of her.

Amazing. Day after day, this woman threw herself at Joseph. Yet he did the right thing—even when no one was looking and even though it cost him his freedom. Why? Because God was watching. As it turns out, he's always watching: "For God will bring every deed into judgment, including the hidden thing, whether it is good or evil."[48]

And what became of Joseph? God blessed him for his obedience. Not only did he get out of jail, he got a job with Potiphar's boss—the Pharaoh himself. In fact, the Pharaoh put Joseph in charge of all of Egypt, making him the second most powerful man in the kingdom. It always pays to do the right thing.

If Joseph were to define character, I think he'd say it's doing the right thing regardless of

---

[47] Genesis 39:12.
[48] Ecclesiastes 12:14.

the cost. Even when no one is looking. In fact, if you want to learn something about yourself, here's a test: What do you do when no one is looking? It will tell you most of what you need to know about your character. For everything else, consider what you do when everyone is looking.

Billy the Kid

What do you do when people are watching? Do you ever make the unpopular choice because it's the right thing to do? Even when everyone thinks you're nuts? That's the other side of character, and Cameron, I'm happy to say you have it. If you don't believe me, just ask Billy.

It was time to choose up sides for the daily scrimmage at baseball camp. You were one of the captains, chosen less for your baseball prowess than your leadership ability. You had the first pick. As usual, little Billy was cowering in the back, expecting to be the last choice. You see Billy wasn't a popular kid. He was a head shorter than the other boys, and his baseball skills were lacking. And to everyone's great amusement, Billy kicked his legs up to the side when he ran, kind of like Forest Gump. Even the adults laughed at the sight. Four-foot-tall Billy was the perennial last pick.

And then there was Tony, the stud of 10-year-old boys' baseball. Tony was cocky, but he had the skills to back it up. No doubt, Tony was the real deal—and he knew it.

Well, before you could clear your throat to announce your first pick, Tony began to strut over to your side like a peacock in full plumage. He naturally presumed that he would be the first pick, as always. You should have seen the look on Tony's face when you announced Billy as your first choice. The only person more surprised than Tony was Billy. He must have felt six-feet tall when he trotted over to your side as the first round draft choice.

That's the other side of character, Cameron. Making an unpopular choice—even when everyone is looking—because it's the right thing to do. I guess that's why you were chosen to be a captain. Character trumps skill every time.

Borrowing from Peter

The final components of your code of conduct are honesty and integrity. Honesty is simply telling the truth. Integrity is doing what you say you're going to do. Not just talking the talk, but walking the walk. The Apostle Peter knew all about honesty and integrity.

Jesus famously predicted that Peter would deny him three times before the rooster crowed. "Never!" Peter exclaimed. But alas, Peter's actions didn't match his words. When the going got tough, he denied he ever knew Christ—not once, but thrice.

Fortunately for Christendom, Peter eventually grew some integrity. As one of the leaders of the early church, he became a man who could be trusted even in the most difficult of situations. And he expected the same of others.

Like Peter, the first followers of Christ sold their possessions and gave the proceeds to the church to support one another. One couple who signed on for this gig was Ananias and Sapphira. Unfortunately for them, they decided to pull a fast one. You see, they sold a piece of land, but held back some of the proceeds. That wouldn't have been so bad, but they lied about it to Peter and the other apostles. Peter wasn't fooled though. "What made you think of doing such a thing?" he admonished Ananias. "You have not lied to men but to God." When Ananias heard this, he fell down and died![49]

A few hours later, Ananias' wife Sapphira came in, not knowing what had happened. Peter asked her, "Tell me, is this the price you and Ananias got for the land?" "Yes," she said, "that is the price." Wrong answer. Sapphira dropped dead on the spot, following her husband to the grave.[50]

---

[49] Acts 5:4.
[50] Acts 5:7-10.

Note that it wasn't lack of generosity that killed Ananias and Sapphira; it was lack of honesty and integrity. They didn't do what they said they would, and to make matters worse, they lied about it. Lying always makes matters worse. Billionaire Martha Stewart didn't go to jail for insider trading. She went to jail for lying about it under oath. That's the way it frequently happens. The underlying offense may be bad, but if the person had just come clean, the punishment would have been far less severe.

And even if you don't get caught, a lie is still a lie. Not just to man, but to God. God takes honesty and integrity seriously. One day you will have to answer for your actions—if not in this life, in the next. And remember, God is always watching.

Journal

9/16/05

Cam,

We had a little situation today. It was almost time for your baseball game, and Mom asked if you finished your homework. You told her you had. She later checked your backpack and discovered you hadn't. Mom and I are sticklers about honesty. Not doing your homework was bad, but lying about it was worse.

In considering your punishment, we debated pulling you from your baseball game. But we realized that we would be punishing your teammates as well. So we settled on having you write 100 times, "Thou Shalt not lie."

"Cameron," I said in my most solemn voice, "do you understand what you did wrong?"

"Yes, sir," you responded, your lower lip quivering.

"Do you understand why we're punishing you?"

"Yes, sir."

"Do you have any questions?"

"Yes, sir."

"You do?" I asked in disbelief, wondering what could possibly be ambiguous. "What's your question?"

"How do you spell 'shalt'?"

It's tough to be mad at you, Cam.
You're a great kid.

I love you,

Dad

Ping Golf Clubs—Part II

So there I was, sitting on the couch, staring at my receipt, debating whether to call the obnoxious golf shop owner to tell him he undercharged me. The mere thought of it was painful. I'd like to tell you I was thinking of biblical heroes like Joseph or Peter, but I wasn't.

I was thinking of Bobby.

It was the final playoff of golf's 1925 U.S. Open, and Bobby Jones' drive ended up in the rough. As he set up to play his second shot, the blade of his iron caused his ball to move ever so slightly. But no one saw it. To everyone's shock and amazement, Bobby turned to the marshals and told them what happened. They discussed the unusual event among themselves and even questioned spectators to see if anyone had seen the ball move. They hadn't. So the marshals left the decision to Bobby. Maybe he was mistaken. Maybe he only imagined that his ball had moved. With the outcome of the U.S. Open hanging in the balance, Bobby held his fate in his own hands. No one had seen the ball move.

But Bobby saw it. And so did God.

What did Bobby do? He called a two-stroke penalty on himself! He lost the championship by one stroke.

Later, when he was praised for his integrity, he responded, "You may as well praise a man for not robbing a bank." Today, the USGA's sportsmanship award is named for Bobby Jones.

So I picked up the phone and called the golf shop. "Hello," the owner answered.

"Hi, it's Spencer Silverglate. I'm the guy who bought the Ping clubs earlier today."

"Yeah, I remember you," he responded. "We don't take returns. You should have tried them out before you bought them."

"I'm not calling to return them," I explained. "I'm calling because you charged me the wrong amount."

"Look, I told you," he barked. "The clubs were already discounted."

"I know," I responded. "What I mean is, you didn't charge me enough."

Dead silence.

"What?" he finally asked in disbelief.

"Yeah, you forgot to charge me for the bag," I said.

After a check of his records, the golf shop owner recognized his error. With an uncharacteristic mixture of humility and gratitude, he said he would split the difference with me. I accepted.

When you do the right thing, I guess it's contagious.

Your Code of Conduct

So here's your code of conduct, Cameron.

Do the right thing regardless of the cost. Even when no one is looking. Even when everyone is looking. And if you're ever in doubt about what the right thing is, just remember the Golden Rule: Love your neighbor as yourself. Who's your neighbor? Everyone, including your enemies.[51] In every situation, consider how you would want to be treated if you were the other person, and the answer will become clear.

Always tell the truth and do what you say you're going to do. If circumstances conspire to prevent you from keeping a promise, admit your mistake and ask for forgiveness. Do it fast, before they find out from someone else. If you follow

---

[51] Matthew 5:38-48.

these simple rules, you'll be a man of character. You'll be that rare person who can be trusted.

Now that you have a code of conduct, let's talk about showing up.

Lesson Five

Most of Life is About Showing Up

"Build me a son, O Lord, who will be strong enough to know when he his weak, and brave enough to face himself when he is afraid, one who will be proud and unbending in honest defeat, and humble and gentle in victory."

—Douglas MacArthur

"80% of success is showing up."

—Woody Allen

Funeral for a Friend

"But I'm swamped this afternoon," I told Kat. "Plus, Joe and I are only acquaintances. Don't you think his dad's funeral is really for family and close friends? I never even met his father."

"Whatever you think," Kat replied.

When I didn't respond after several minutes, she pursued the issue as I knew she would. "Let me ask you this," she said as I waited for the counter-punch. "How would you advise someone who asked you what to do in that situation?"

Ugghh, a right hook to the body.

"I don't know," I stammered. "I guess I'd tell 'em to show up."

"Hmm, that sounds like good counsel," she replied.

So there I was, pulling into Menorah Gardens Funeral Home at 1 p.m. on a Friday afternoon. It must have been 95 degrees in the shade. And there wasn't any shade. The service was outside in the sweltering heat—perfect weather for a bathing suit and a floppy hat, not a business suit and a yarmulke.

As I approached the procession of family and friends, I spotted Joe. He was gaunt and unshaven. It was obvious he hadn't slept in days. But he was still Joe, affable as always. Smiling, laughing, trying to make everyone else feel better. And then he caught a glimpse of me. His countenance turned grim, and tears began to roll down his cheeks. Oh boy, I thought, this could get messy. Maybe I should have stayed home after all.

"Hey man," I said as I offered Joe my outstretched hand. Joe didn't take my hand; he hugged me. And then he really began to sob. It was awkward. I didn't know what to do, so I just hugged him back. But he wouldn't let me go. He just kept crying. So I whispered in his ear, "I know. I know what it's like to lose a father."

Joe choked back his tears, composed himself as best he could, and said "that's not why I'm crying. I'm crying because you showed up . . ."

Then I started to cry.

Joe and I have had some deep spiritual conversations over the years, ones in which I shared my Christian faith with him. Maybe that's why he was so moved. Or maybe it was because, unlike his relatives, I didn't have to show up. And I almost didn't.

Joe went on to deliver an amazing eulogy for his father. It was moving. It was humorous. It was honoring and courageous. It was a proper and fitting tribute to a father, delivered by the only person in the world who could do it—his son. That Joe summoned the strength to give it was nothing short of supernatural.

Looking into the eyes of his widowed mother, his sister and his young children, Joe explained that death is part of life. As he lifted the first shovel of dirt over the six-foot deep burial chamber, he instructed his 13-year-old son to be strong. Not to look away, but to listen to the sound as the dirt fell onto the coffin. He said it was a sound he'd never forget; a sound he would hear again when he turned the shovel over Joe's grave. With that, Joe dropped the dirt into the tomb. As it hit the coffin, the silence was pierced with a loud, echoing thud.

It was a sound I'll never forget. I hear it all the time in my head, and it reminds me to show up. To live life to the fullest—before the dirt falls on my coffin.

It's really astonishing when I think back on it. I saw a man transformed in minutes from a weeping wreck into John Rambo. I don't think I could have done what Joe did that afternoon, not if it had been my father's funeral. Joe later told me he was inspired because I showed up and because of the words of encouragement I gave him before his eulogy. Nothing magical; I just told him he could do it.

And me, what did I get out of it? I'll tell you what. I got to meet God that day. I was used by the King of the Universe to minister to a friend in need. There's no better feeling in the world.

One of the best decisions I ever made was showing up that day. Not just for Joe, but also for me. That's true for most of life—it's about showing up.

An Inconvenient Truth

Showing up is never convenient. Attending a funeral for the relative of a friend. Visiting a colleague in the hospital. Stopping for the guy broken down on the side of the road. Spending time with an elderly relative. Serving the homeless. Mentoring a young person. Assisting a handicapped person. Helping a friend in need. Taking time to connect with service people—the waiter, the maid, the mail carrier, the gardener, the locker room attendant. Attending your son's band recital or golf match or baseball game. Sharing the gospel with a stranger. It's all inconvenient, but it's necessary. Showing up makes all the difference in life. Because when you do, God usually shows up too.

Meeting God

How far would you go to help a friend? Two thousand years ago, four friends heard that Jesus was in town. They had a fifth friend, a paralytic, whose only hope of ever walking again was to see Jesus. The problem was that the whole town had the same idea. The event was standing room only, with folks lining up outside the door just to catch a glimpse of the Messiah.

The friends couldn't get near the door, but they were undeterred. They climbed on top of the house, cut a hole in the roof and lowered their friend through it. When Jesus saw their faith, he healed their paralyzed friend—both physically and spiritually. "Son, your sins are forgiven," he said. "Get up, take your mat and go home."[52]

Amazing. The faith of the man's friends and their willingness to go out of their way to help made it possible for him not just to walk, but to soar forever into eternity. And what did the friends get out of it? They got to meet God! Imagine how their own faith must have exploded when they saw their paralyzed companion pick up his mat and walk home!

That's the way it usually works when you show up. You meet God in the process.

When Opportunity Knocks

The other side of showing up is first recognizing and then seizing opportunities when they arise—the baseball try-out, the job interview, the business deal, the social invitation, the mission trip, the new relationship. I think the reason we sometimes shy away from opportunities like these is not because they're inconvenient, but

---

[52] Mark 2:1-12.

because they're scary. It's fear that prevents us from seizing the opportunity.

What do we fear? You name it. We fear failing. We fear looking foolish. We fear rejection. Losing money. Losing friends. Just plain losing. We fear getting hurt—emotionally and physically. We fear dying. We fear risk. We fear the unknown.

Yes, we are much afraid. And our fear keeps us form showing up; from pursuing opportunities and realizing our God-given potential. Don't just take my word for it. Here's what some other folks have said about fear and opportunity, risk and reward:

> "The secret of success in life is for a man to be ready for his opportunity when it comes."
>
> —Benjamin Disraeli

> "You miss 100% of the shots you never take."
>
> —Wayne Gretzky

> "There is a tide in the affairs of men, Which, taken at the flood, leads on to fortune; Omitted, all the voyage of their life Is bound in shallows and in miseries."
>
> —William Shakespeare
> *Julius Caesar*, Act IV, scene iii

"Ultimately, we know deeply that the other side of every fear is freedom."

—Marilyn Ferguson

"There is no security in life; there is only opportunity."

—Douglas MacArthur

"No pain, no gain."

—Arnold Schwarzenegger

"Progress always involves risk. You can't steal second base and keep your foot on first."

—Frederick B. Wilcox

"Cowards die many times before their deaths; The valiant taste death but once."

—William Shakespeare
Julius Caesar, Act II, scene ii

"FEAR is False Evidence Appearing Real."

—Anonymous

"Pain pays."

—Lance Armstrong

"Courage. What makes a King out of a slave? Courage. What makes the flag on the mast to wave? Courage. What makes the elephant charge his tusk in the misty mist or the dusky dusk? What makes the muskrat guard his musk? Courage. What makes the Sphinx the 7th Wonder? Courage. What makes the dawn come up like THUNDER?! Courage. What makes the Hottentot so hot? What puts the "ape" in ape-ricot? Whatta they got that I ain't got? Courage!"

—Cowardly Lion,
Wizard of Oz

"Let me assert my firm belief that the only thing we have to fear is fear itself—nameless, unreasoning, unjustified terror which paralyzes needed effort to convert retreat into advance."

—Franklin D. Roosevelt
Inaugural Address, March 4, 1933

Yet, if all we have to fear is fear itself, why are we so afraid? We know that fear is illogical, that the things we fear almost never come to pass. We know too that we will fail to succeed in 100% of the things we don't try. Still, we can't seem to overcome our fear.

I've been afraid of many things in my life. Most notably, I've been afraid of public speaking, which presents a bit of a problem for a trial lawyer. I tried logic, meditation, visualization, deep breathing exercises. You name it, I tried it. Nothing worked. Until one day, like Jonas Salk discovering the cure for polio, I stumbled over it—the antidote for fear. The one sure-fire thing that really works. And now I'm willing to share it with you, my son.

The Cure for Fear

The cure for fear is showing up. Sorry, but there's no mystery to it. No secret incantation. No magic pill. No therapeutic elixir. It's doing the thing you're afraid of—again, and again and again. Until eventually, you're no longer afraid. Like the Nike commercial says, "Just do it."

I've learned that courage is not the absence of fear. It's proceeding—with hands trembling and knees shaking—in spite of fear. Yes, it's exactly backwards. We want courage before we face our fears, but it doesn't work that way. We build our courage *by* facing our fears. We have to do the deed first; the courage comes afterwards. It is the fruit of our willingness, our obedience, our action.

That's how it was with me and public speaking. I just kept doing it, and doing it, and doing it—not without fear, but in spite of my fear. One joke at a time. One toast at a time. One story at a time. One deposition. One hearing. One speech. One trial. One sermon. Until, eventually, I was no longer afraid. I became brave through repetition.

So here's my advice: If you want to overcome your fear, just keep showing up.

WHOM SHALL I FEAR?

The last thing I want to tell you about fear is focus. When you're afraid, ask yourself this: What am I focusing on? It's probably your fear. Just ask Peter.

It was late at night, and the disciples were in a boat on the Sea of Galilee. The wind and waves came up like a hurricane. Then Jesus strolled up, walking on the water of all things. The disciples thought he was a ghost, and they were afraid. But Jesus said to them: "Take courage! It is I. Don't be afraid."[53]

The sight of the Lord must have emboldened Peter. He asked the Lord to make him a waterwalker too. "Come," said Jesus. And Peter did—he walked on water! But in a weak moment, Peter took his eyes off Christ. He focused on the wind and the waves, and he began to sink. "You

---
[53] Matthew 14:27.

of little faith," Jesus said as he saved Peter. "Why did you doubt?"[54]

Isn't that exactly the way it is with us? When we focus on our fears, they overwhelm us. But when we focus on God, our fears become small. When we focus on God's agenda instead of our own, our stress dissolves. When we can honestly say to our heavenly father, "Thy kingdom come, thy will be done,"[55] our struggles are placed in proper perspective.

So Cameron, here's the lesson: If you keep your eyes on Christ, you will have nothing to fear. If you follow God's will, he will give you courage.

I saved the best quote about fear for last. It's by my boy, King David.

> "The Lord is my light and my salvation—
> Whom shall I fear?
> The Lord is the stronghold of my life—
> Of whom shall I be afraid?"[56]

Whom will you fear, Cameron? Of what will you be afraid? What will you do when the hurricane blows into your life?

---

[54] Matthew 14:31.
[55] Matthew 6:9-13 (the Lord's Prayer).
[56] Psalm 27:1.

The Hurricane

11/11/01

Cam,

It took you six years of life, but you finally did it. You're as tall as the wooden pirate at Boomers amusement park. Today would be the day you would take on the Hurricane—the only wooden roller coaster in Florida. $10 per person, unlimited rides.

You were scared out of your mind. After all the waiting and anticipation, when the day finally came, you didn't want to ride at all. After a pep talk, you eventually got your courage up. You said you'd do it if I sat next to you. I must admit, that made me feel pretty good.

So we buckled the seat belt and pulled the bar across our laps. You were terrified. I put my arm around you and held you tight. We began to move, slowly at first, then faster. Up the first mountainous climb, down the first sheer drop. Our stomachs jumped into our throats. A look of shock and awe swept across your face. Around the hairpin turns we went, tossed and turned in every direction. Your knuckles were white from your death-grip on the safety bar. Until finally, mercifully, the ride was over.

You rose from your seat and wobbled to your feet. Several moments of stunned silence passed. It seemed as if you were stricken mute. Then suddenly you spoke: "Let's do it again, Daddy."

And we did. Again and again and again. After a couple of rides, you didn't want me to put my arm around you anymore. By the fifth ride, you had your hands in the air. When we were ready to leave, you wanted to ride all by yourself. I drew the line there.

You conquered a Hurricane today, Cameron. You were afraid, but you did it anyway—in spite of your fear. Until eventually, you weren't afraid. It seemed like you were growing up right before my eyes. And you were. It made me appreciate that the time you're going to need me to hold you is short and precious. I'm going to savor every minute of it.

I love you,

Dad

Showing Up

So that's what most of life is about—showing up. Showing up when it's inconvenient. Showing up when you're afraid. Showing up no matter what. Because when you show up, you meet God in the process.

Keep showing up, Cameron. And keep your eyes on Christ. If you can do that, you'll have nothing to fear.

Now, if you're going to show up, you need to know what to do when you get there. You need to know about heart.

Lesson Six

Whatever You Choose to Do, Do it with All Your Heart

"Catch on fire with enthusiasm, and people will come for miles to watch you burn."

—John Wesley

"Life is not a journey to the grave with intentions of arriving safely in a pretty, well-preserved body, but rather to skid in broadside, thoroughly used up, totally worn out and loudly proclaiming... Wow! What a ride!"

—Anonymous

Heartless in Miami

I was a born quitter.

Whatever I started, I quit. Little league baseball? Quit. Boy Scouts? Quit. Religious School? Quit. High school wrestling? Quit. Summer jobs? Quit. College Fraternity? Quit. Relationships? Quit.

When the going got tough, I quit.

When I was 14 years old, I decided to try out for the 130-pound Pop Warner tackle football team with my nephew and lifelong friend Russell. We had absolutely no idea what we were in for.

The weeks of workouts preceding the first game were like nothing we had experienced. It was summertime in Miami. To say it was hot would be like calling a kidney stone uncomfortable. And to make matters worse, the coach was a full fledged, card-carrying sadist. It was back in the day when coaches didn't let kids drink water during practice. If you got heat stroke, you were a sissy. If you couldn't get up after a play, you were dogging it.

It was a summer of firsts for Russell and me. It was the first time we ever ran wind sprints. The first time we ever had full-contact practices. The first time that death seemed like a reasonable option.

Sure, it was tough on the rest of the boys, but they seemed to have way more football experience. Somehow, they were able to withstand the torture. Some even thrived on it. As for Russell and me, we prayed every day that practice would be rained out. It never was.

Finally, the summer wound down, and the first game was in sight.

Then the unthinkable happened.

The league administrators were checking birth certificates to make sure that all the boys were the correct age for their respective teams. Coach pulled me aside and told me I wasn't. It seems that I was a couple of months too old for the 130-pound team—even though I was maybe 115 pounds soaking wet. If I was going to play football, it would be with the 145-pound monsters. From my vantage point, they might as well have been the 1972 Dolphins. I wasn't in their league. To make matters worse, my buddy Russell, six months my junior, would be staying with the 130-pounders.

"Son, if you love the game of football—if you've got heart—you'll do whatever it takes to play," Coach said. "Even if it means playing with the 145-pound team."

I thought about what Coach said, and then I showed him what I was made of.

I quit.

WHERE'S YOUR HEART?

I spent much of my life wandering aimlessly from activity to activity. I had no direction, no passion, no commitment. I'm not talking about "showing up" for the occasional obligation. My parents made sure I did that. I'm talking about the significant things that I chose to do in a particular season of my life—sports, extracurricular activities, school, work, relationships, religion. To this day, it pains me to say it. I had no heart. And I came to learn that I wasn't alone. As it turns out, lots of folks are walking around with hollow chests.

I've often observed that ski resorts are packed with people at the bottom and middle of the mountain, but almost empty at the top. It's the same way in life. In every organization, there's a logjam at the bottom and middle, but it's always lonely at the top. It's why the front row in every classroom, church, temple and seminar is virtually empty. People race to sit in the middle. It's why churches fill up on Easter and Christmas and synagogues on Yom Kippur and Rosh Hashanah. Where are the faithful the rest of the year? We're a species satisfied by mediocrity. Commitment is just too, well . . . committal.

It seems to start when we're kids. In classrooms and sports fields across the country, a precious few kids give everything they've got. The majority get by on 70% effort. They seem to be afraid to apply themselves. Maybe they think that if they fail, they'll have a ready made excuse—"I didn't even try."

The problem is that these kids eventually become adults, and the same apathy that plagued them on the sports field and in the classroom follows them to their work. They never commit to a job, always having one foot in and one foot out. They sleepwalk through work like they sleepwalk through life. Their resumés are perennially updated and ready to be sent to the next prospective employer, where the grass always seems greener. One day, they suppose, they'll find the dream job, the one for which they were born. But the next job never seems to be what it was cracked up to be. So they keep looking.

Then there are those who won't commit to a relationship. The serial daters who are never ready to settle down. After all, someone better might be just around the corner. And then there are the couples who have been together for years. They share property, occasionally pets and sometimes even children. But still they won't pull the trigger and get married. That would be way too much commitment.

Others commit to marriage in name only. They pledge that they're in it for better or worse, richer or poorer, sickness and health—only until death will they part. Or until they fall out of love. Or the bills pile up. Or they meet someone else. Then it's over. About half of all marriages end in divorce.

Finally, there are those who won't commit to God. I'm not talking about atheists—at least they've taken a stand. I'm talking about the people who have a general belief in a supernatural being who has little involvement in their day-to-day lives. Theirs is a small god, called upon in times of need, but otherwise sitting on the shelf next to their other idols.

And the Bible? Nothing more than a collection of man-made fables. Sure, some of the stories and admonitions teach timeless wisdom, but others are outdated relics. Certainly, the Bible has no authority over their modern lives. Their attitude toward God is neither hot nor cold. These folks meander through life in a state of tepid indifference toward their creator.

I know all of these people quite well. After all, I was one of them.

BURNING THE SHIPS

One night not too long ago I couldn't sleep and found myself watching the History Channel. It was 1519, and the Spanish Conquistador Hernando Cortez set out to conquer Mexico with only 10 ships and 617 men. With an ocean separating him from his homeland, Cortez did the unthinkable. He burned his own ships! Crazy? Deranged? Nope. Cortez knew exactly what he was doing. With the odds stacked decidedly against them, he removed all thought of retreat from his men. They would either succeed, or they would die trying. Turning back was not on option.

I laid awake that night wondering if I had ever applied that level of commitment in my life. An endeavor where I never considered turning back. As I pondered the question, I concluded that I had. When my father died in my freshman year of college, things changed. I changed. For the first time in my life, I was on my own. It was sink or swim time. I would have to quit quitting. It was time to stop playing around and start committing.

And commit I did. I committed to school. I gave it 100%. I committed to exercise. After more than 30 years, I still work out almost every day. I committed to a relationship. I met Kat when I was 19, and she's the only woman I have ever loved. I committed to work. I've been a lawyer for over 20 years, and counting. And I committed to you, Cameron. Since you were born, I've poured everything I had into being the best Dad I could be.

Like Cortez, I burned the ships of retreat in my life. I realized that the key to success was commitment. But success to what end? Cortez wanted gold and glory. What did I want? What was the point of all this commitment? I was in a quandary. Somehow, I had missed something.

Working for the Lord

The puzzle piece I was missing all those years was God. Success for the sake of success was unsatisfying. Empty. Meaningless. Without him, all my striving was in vain. So in 1998, I made the ultimate commitment. I surrendered my life to Jesus Christ. I committed to God and have been trying to learn about him ever since. It turns out that he has a lot to say about commitment.

Commitment at Work. We were made to work. The Book of Genesis says, "The Lord God took the man and put him in the Garden of Eden to work it and take care of it."[57] From the very beginning, God intended us to work.

And not only to work, but to work with gusto. "Whatever you do, work at it with all your heart, as working for the Lord, not for men, since you know that you will receive an inheritance from the Lord as a reward. It is the Lord Christ you are serving."[58]

Notice that the scripture does not describe the perfect job. It says "whatever" you do, work at it with "all" your heart. God is less concerned with what we do than who we do it for and how

---

[57] Genesis 2:15.
[58] Colossians 3:23-24.

we do it. And he doesn't approve of slacking in the workplace. Why? Because we honor God when we perform our jobs with excellence. From God's vantage point, we're working for him, not our earthly bosses. And as Christians, we are Christ's representatives on earth. When we give 100% effort at work—especially on the unpleasant assignments—people will want to know what makes us tick. Our attitude at work is a great tool to share Christ.

Commitment in Marriage. The Book of Genesis also talks about marriage: "[A] man will leave his father and mother and be united to his wife, and they will become one flesh."[59] From the looks of it, God didn't intend us to play the field. He made us to go through life two-by-two. Husband and wife. One flesh. One love. Forever.

And divorce? "'I hate divorce,' says the Lord God of Israel."[60] If that's not clear enough, here's what Jesus said on the subject: "But I tell you that anyone who divorces his wife, except for marital unfaithfulness, causes her to become an adulteress, and anyone who marries the divorced woman commits adultery."[61]

God intended us to be together in marriage forever.[62]

---

[59] Genesis 2:24.
[60] Malachi 2:16.
[61] Matthew 5:31-32.
[62] Some people renounce marriage to spend more time working for God's kingdom. According to Jesus, this is

Commitment to God. "Love the Lord your God with all your heart and with all your soul and with all your mind."[63] This is the first and greatest commandment. God doesn't want half our hearts. He's a jealous God; he wants the whole thing.

This is how Jesus put it in the Book of Revelation: "I know your deeds, that you are neither cold nor hot. I wish you were either one or the other! So, because you are lukewarm—neither hot nor cold—I am about to spit you out of my mouth."[64]

Isn't it amazing? Here is the God of the Universe telling us to fish or cut bait. He wants us either hot or cold. All in or all out. He doesn't want a slice. He doesn't want a percentage. He wants the whole thing. It's like the joke about ham and eggs—the chicken is involved, but the pig is committed. God doesn't want involvement. He wants total and complete commitment. He wants us to burn our ships.

Of course, God isn't much different than people when it comes to commitment. We all want the same thing. Every teacher wants a committed student. Every coach wants a committed player. Every boss wants a committed employee. Every man and woman wants a committed spouse. Every parent wants a committed child. Every kid wants a committed parent. Everyone

---

appropriate. See Matthew 19:11-12.
[63] Matthew 22:37.
[64] Revelation 3:15-16.

on the receiving end craves commitment. The question is, will we be committed on the giving end?

Even though we all want commitment from others, we don't always give it ourselves. Yet that's exactly what God expects from each of us—commitment in every aspect of our lives, especially to him. It may be rare, but I've seen it. Some people have that level of commitment.

The Heart of a Champion

The hope of redemption was palpable. The defending national champion Florida Gators finished the 2007 football season with a disappointing 9-4 record. But that was all behind them at the start of 2008, especially after dispatching Hawaii, Miami and Tennessee in their first three games. The next victim was the perennial SEC doormat, Mississippi, at home, in the "Swamp." Las Vegas odds had Florida winning by 22. The spread seemed low.

The only problem was that Ole Miss didn't get the memo; they came to win. The mighty Gators found themselves down 31-24 with only 5:26 left in the fourth quarter. As if on cue, Florida came back and scored a touchdown. Only an extra point—football's equivalent to a chip shot—was needed to tie the game. Then the unthinkable happened. The kick was blocked.

The Gators weren't dead yet though. They got the ball back and advanced to the Ole Miss 32 yard line. It was fourth-and-one, with only 41 seconds left on the clock. To no one's surprise, the Gators went with their fool-proof, never miss, short-yardage play—Heisman Trophy-winning quarterback Tim Tebow up the middle. The noise in the Swamp was deafening as Tebow lowered his shoulder, ran head-on into the Ole Miss defensive line . . . and was stopped short of the first down.

90,000 fans stood in stunned silence, unable to accept that their superman was mortal after all. Ole Miss regained possession and ran out the clock. Mississippi 31, Florida 30.

Although some might consider it historic that Florida lost to Mississippi that day, the real history was made after the game. In a speech now etched in stone on the wall at Ben Hill Griffin Stadium (literally), Tim Tebow, fighting back tears, said these words:

THE PROMISE

> To the fans and everybody in Gator Nation, I'm sorry. I'm extremely sorry. We were hoping for an undefeated season. That was my goal, something Florida has never done here.

> I promise you one thing, a lot of good will come out of this. You will never see any player in the entire country play as hard as I will play the rest of the season. You will never see someone push the rest of the team as hard as I will push everybody the rest of the season. You will never see a team play harder than we will the rest of the season.
>
> God bless.
>
> —Tim Tebow
> September 27, 2008

What happened afterwards? Exactly what Tebow promised. No one worked harder than the Gators as they went on to win all of their remaining games and captured their second national title in three seasons.

What impresses me about this story is not Tebow's talent, but his commitment. His determination. His heart. Anyone who's watched him play has noticed the scriptures etched in the eye black he wears on his face during games. Tebow knows whom he's fighting for.

Home-schooled by missionary parents, Tebow is a devout Christian. In March 2008, while his classmates and teammates took off for spring break, Tebow traveled to his father's orphanage in the Philippines. The same year, he also went on mission trips to Croatia and Thailand, all while maintaining a 3.68 GPA.

Why work so hard? Why not just focus on football? This is how Tebow explained it: "I want to do everything in my power that football gives me to influence as many people as I can for the good, because that's going to mean so much more when it's all said and done than just playing football."[65]

So inspired was Coach Urban Meyer by his star player's commitment to God and his dedication to excellence on and off the field that he took his own family on a mission trip to the Dominican Republic. "Tim has done a lot of things that have opened my eyes," Meyer said. "To have our children experience that . . . was a life-changing experience. It's something we're going to, if possible, do every year."[66]

When you work for the Lord, and you do it with all your heart, people can see it in you. It's like John Wesley said, "Catch on fire with enthusiasm, and people will come for miles to watch you burn." And the best part is that the enthusiasm is contagious. Like a fire, it spreads.

---

[65] Mark Long, The Detroit News, Aug. 28, 2008.
[66] Id.

There's Something Different About Him

5/4/08

Cam,

Last Tuesday was the annual awards ceremony for middle school. I rushed to the event straight from work, just in time for the 7 p.m. start. You received awards for science fair and speech, as we expected. I contemplated leaving early to go home and eat and maybe catch the end of Dancing with the Stars.

Mom made me stay.

For the next hour-and-a-half, I sat through awards for every subject. Math—Becky Thomas. English—Becky Thomas. Science—Becky Thomas. Fine Arts—are you kidding me?—Becky Thomas. "And the award for best all around student goes to . . ." You guessed it. Becky Thomas.

My mind began to drift. "Why isn't Cameron getting any of the 'real' awards? If he only applied himself, they would be calling his name instead of that Thomas girl.

Who does she think she is, anyway? Hmmm, maybe it's not really Cameron's fault. Maybe it's our fault that we didn't give him better genes. No, that's impossible. The bad genes must have come from Kat."

And then, just when I was becoming delusional from hunger, the principal announced the grand finale. The Patriot Award. The award for the one student in the entire seventh grade who best exemplified the ideals of the school: excellence in academics, in sports, in citizenship and in character.

Darned if she didn't call Cameron Silverglate!

I almost fell out of my chair. The only one in the auditorium more surprised than me was you. Of course, Mom expected you to win.

It was a great evening, but the epilogue is even better. A couple days later, Becky Thomas's mother called Mom to ask her advice. She said that Becky had been asking deep spiritual questions, and she didn't know quite how to answer them. She saw something different in you and in our family. She thought we might have some answers.

It's like your golf coach said the night of the Patriot Award, "There's just something different about Cameron." Of course, we know what it is.

Cam, I don't care if you're ever the most outstanding student. All I care about is that you keep letting God shine through you. One day, when your trophies are in the closet collecting dust, his light will still be shining bright. It will shine for all eternity.

Dad

Have Heart

Well, that's the lesson about heart, one of the most important human qualities. It trumps skill. It's better than talent. It beats intelligence. I'd always take a person with grit and determination over one with ability but no passion. Anyone would.

I'll wrap up the lesson with a few verses from one of my favorite songs:

The Motions[67]

This might hurt
It's not safe

But I know that I've got to make a change
I don't care if I break
At least I'll be feeling something
'Cause just okay is not enough
Help me fight through the nothingness of life

I don't wanna go through the motions
I don't wanna go one more day
Without your all consuming passion inside of me
I don't want to spend my whole life asking,
'What if I had given everything?'
Instead of going through the motions

Cameron, don't spend your life wondering what it would be like if you committed. Don't just go through the motions. Whatever you choose to do, do it with all your heart. Burn the ships and go all in. Not because you're working for an earthly prize, but an eternal one. Trust me, people are watching you.

Now, if you're ready to commit, you need to be careful what you decide to pursue.

---

[67] *The Motions*, written by Matthew West (2008), from the *Something to Say* album.

LESSON SEVEN

WORLDLY PURSUITS WILL NEVER SATISFY YOU COMPLETELY

"MONEY NEVER MADE A MAN HAPPY YET, NOR WILL IT. THE MORE A MAN HAS, THE MORE HE WANTS. INSTEAD OF FILLING A VACUUM, IT MAKES ONE."

—BENJAMIN FRANKLIN

"POOR MAN WANNA BE RICH,
RICH MAN WANNA BE KING
AND A KING AINT SATISFIED
TILL HE RULES EVERYTHING."

—BRUCE SPRINGSTEEN, *BADLANDS*

SWEET LORETTA

You never forget your first love. Mine was Loretta. Sweet Lortetta.

My heart raced when we were together. My mind drifted when we were apart.

I drew pictures of Loretta, wrote songs about Loretta, dreamt of Loretta.

My love was all encompassing.

But Dad never approved of Loretta. "Too old," he would say. "Been around the block too many times. One of those fast ones. You're gonna get hurt."

Dad was probably right. But when you're in love, logic is the first casualty. And I was in deep.

Then, one day, tragedy.

It wasn't her fault really. A lapse of concentration was all. My neighbor, just driving down the street. A momentary distraction.

A skid. A swerve. A scream.

Then shock and horror.

Loretta was hit. It was fatal.

I sobbed uncontrollably when they came to take Loretta away . . . to the junkyard.

And so ended my love affair with Loretta—my first car.

What Are You Striving For?

Yes, I was in love with a car. A 1970 Chevelle Super Sport to be exact. Black with white racing stripes. Faster than stink. It was the sweetest ride around. I spent the entire summer of my 16th year bussing tables just to have it painted. I loved that car. But I don't think it loved me back. Half the time it didn't even start. And, like all material things, it ended up in the junk heap.

No matter. Other things took its place. Coins, clothes, watches. Gear of all kinds. Eventually, houses.

And then there's money itself. It's not that I love money, but let's just say we're dating.

So what about you? Be honest. What has your affection? What's got your attention? What are you striving for?

One way to answer these questions is to consider where you spend your money. As Jesus said, "For where your treasure is, there your heart will be also."[68] If you want to find your heart, just follow your money. Take a look at your last credit card bill and bank statement. They'll lead right to your heart.

The other place your heart lives is your calendar. On what do you spend your time? When

---

[68] Matthew 6:21.

your mind drifts, where does it go? For where you spend your time and focus your attention, there you heart will be also (that one was me).

Here are some options:

Money. Jesus spent more time talking about money than virtually any other subject. He knew it can get a hold of us like nothing else. For some folks, it's about getting rich. But for most of us, it's about getting just a little bit more. We rationalize that we need to pay our bills. But how did our bills get so big? Who told us that we had to have *that* house and drive *that* car? Who told us to spend more than we earn?

Let me ask you some questions directly. You need money, but how much is enough? How far will you go to get it? And what if you succeed? Will you really be satisfied then?

I know the answers to these questions for my fellow lawyers. We are among the highest paid and most influential of all professionals. Yet studies repeatedly show that we experience some of the highest rates of depression, job dissatisfaction, chemical dependency and divorce. Most of my brothers and sisters in the profession would not become lawyers again if they had the chance and would not recommend the career to their own children. Money and influence clearly are not making us happy.

Stuff. Just a few miles from our house is one of the largest tourist attractions in Florida. Tour buses carrying thousands of visitors arrive weekly. It's not Disney World or Universal Studios. It's Sawgrass Mils, one of the country's largest outlet malls. Thousands of people attend mass there every day, worshipping at the altar of stuff.

If the love of money is the root of all evil, the love of stuff is a close second. Last year in Miami, two teenagers ended up killing a boy in a botched attempt to steel his Sony Play Station Portable. They did it for the stuff.

We read newspaper accounts all the time of people who die protecting their possessions. They're willing to die over stuff.

Okay, you might not kill or die for material things, but how far would you go? How much of your life is consumed by stuff? Working for it, thinking about it, shopping for it, spending on it, maintaining it, insuring it, worrying about it, disposing of it? How much stuff is enough?

Fame. American Idol. America's Got Talent. Dancing with the Stars.

We worship the famous. And we'd do just about anything to become famous ourselves. But if we actually achieved it, how satisfying would it be?

How satisfied were Michael Jackson, Howard Hughes, Ernest Hemingway, Marilyn Monroe, Elvis Presley, Heath Ledger, Janis Joplin, Kurt Kobain, Sigmund Freud, Dana Plato, Freddie Prinze, Keith Moon, Sid Vicious, Hank Williams, David Carradine and Jimi Hendrix? All committed suicide or died of accidental drug overdose.

The original Superman George Reeves shot himself in the head.

British author Virginia Wolf filled her coat pockets with stones, waded into a river and drowned herself.

Actress Peg Entwistle jumped from the "H" in the famous "Hollywood" sign. How ironic. She left a suicide note: "I am afraid, I am a coward. I am sorry for everything. If I had done this along time ago, it would have saved a lot of pain."[69] She was 24.

Fame didn't seem to make any of these folks happy.

Relationships. Eharmony. Match.com. Love-access.com.

Single people want relationships. If they could just find the right person, they'd be eternally happy.

---

[69] "Girl Leaps To Death From Sign," Los Angeles Times, September 9, 1932, p. A1.

How much time and energy is spent looking for Mister or Miss Right? And what if we're lucky enough to find him or her? Will that be the answer to all our problems? Just ask a married couple that question and listen to them laugh. The national divorce rate hovers around fifty percent. Married people have problems, too.

Family. Some people live for family. Their worlds revolve around spouse or parents or kids. It sounds noble, but has devotion to our family left us with a deep sense of fulfillment? Or is something still missing? After all, people are only human. They tend to fall short of expectations. And even if they live up to expectations, people don't last forever. Like taxes, death is guaranteed.

Career. Work, of course, is both necessary and important. Godly, even. Until we worship the career itself rather than the God we're working for. Some people are devoted to their careers above all else. But what if we get the raise, the promotion and corner office? We will be happy then?

Substances. Food. Alcohol. Drugs. Tobacco. We worship substances. They fill a temporary void in our lives, but the feeling never seems to last. Show me the food or drink that satisfies your hunger or quenches your thirst forever. Show me the drug that makes you high for eternity.

Experiences. Some of us live for experiences. Travel. Entertainment. Video games. Parties. Events. Ball games. Adventures. All are fleeting.

Sex. Also an experience, but it deserves a category all by itself. If we could just have enough sexual encounters, we'd be satisfied. But do you know anyone who's slept his way to fulfillment?

Education. Some folks worship at the temple of higher learning. Perhaps they can learn their way into contentment.

Hobbies. How much golf can you play before you're happy? How many fish can you catch until you're satisfied? Show me the hobby that never disappoints and never ends.

Health and Fitness. Working out and eating well is healthy, right? Not when it's your god. I've never heard of anyone jogging into heaven.

Retirement. We'll be happy when we retire and move to the (pick one) mountains, beach, country. Finally, we'll have time to do the things we've always dreamed of. That's not the reality I see, unless you've dreamed of going to doctors' appointments, watching day-time television and driving slowly in the left lane for 20 miles with the turn signal on. Do you know many retirees bubbling over with joy?

The truth is, you're probably striving for at least one of these things. But what will happen if you achieve it?

THEN WHAT?

There's one question that looms larger than all the others on the subject of worldly pursuits. One question that separates the wheat from the chaff. One question from which there's no hiding.

"Then what?"

Here's how it works. Suppose you win the lottery. Then you get the fame and the stuff and the relationships? Then what? Will you be fulfilled?

What if you succeed in attaining a wonderful family, a great career and hard body? Then what? Will you be done striving?

What if you travel to every city in the world, ingest every substance and obtain degrees in every subject from the best universities? Then what? Will you be satisfied?

What if you catch a 20-pound bass, shoot a 59 at St. Andrews, have sex with Carmen Electra and retire early . . . with full benefits? Then what?

What if you get everything you've been striving for your whole life?

Then what?

Fortunately, someone has already answered this question for us.

Three thousand years ago, God appeared to King Solomon when he became King of Israel. "Ask for whatever you want me to give you," God said. Solomon asked for only one thing—wisdom. So pleased was God with this request that he granted Solomon not only wisdom, but also the greatest wealth, riches and honor ever known.[70]

How wise was Solomon? Just read the Book of Proverbs, which Solomon authored, and try not to be impressed. It contains 3,000 of the greatest insights ever written on the human condition.

How rich was Solomon? He had 1,400 of the finest chariots and 1,200 of the best imported horses.[71] Today, that would be like owning over a thousand Ferraris!

But his wealth wasn't limited to transportation. He undertook building projects the likes of which the world had never known, including the great Temple in Jerusalem. Solomon employed 80,000 stone cutters, 70,000 laborers and 3,600 foremen.[72] It took seven years to build the Temple,[73] a drop in the bucket compared to the 13 years it took to build Solomon's own palace.[74]

---

[70] 2 Chronicles 1:7-12.
[71] 2 Chronicles 1:14.
[72] 2 Chronicles 2:17-18.
[73] 1 Kings 6:38.
[74] 1 Kings 7:1.

And Solomon wasn't just another smart, rich guy. He was a lady's man too. He had 700 wives and 300 concubines (women kept around for sexual "companionship").[75] That's a thousand women! One wonders how Solomon had time to rule the kingdom.

So what did Solomon do with his wealth and his fame and his power? He undertook an experiment. A sort of ancient science fair project. His goal? To answer that age-old question: Then what?

What happens when a man gets everything he ever wanted? Will he finally be satisfied?

Solomon reports his findings:

> I thought in my heart, "come now, I will test you with pleasure to find out what is good." But that also proved to be meaningless. "Laughter," I said, "is foolish. And what does pleasure accomplish?" I tried cheering myself with wine, and embracing folly—my mind still guiding me with wisdom. I wanted to see what was worthwhile for men to do under heaven during the few days of their lives.

---

[75] 1 Kings 11:3.

> I undertook great projects: I built houses for myself and planted vineyards. I made gardens and parks and planted all kinds of fruit trees in them. I made reservoirs to water groves of flourishing trees. I bought male and female slaves and had other slaves who were born in my house. I also owned more herds and flocks than anyone in Jerusalem before me. I amassed silver and gold for myself, and the treasure of kings and provinces. I acquired men and women singers, and a harem as well—the delights of the heart of man. I became greater by far than anyone in Jerusalem before me. In all this my wisdom stayed with me.
>
> I denied myself nothing my eyes desired; I refused my heart no pleasure. My heart took delight in all my work, and this was the reward for all my labor. Yet when I surveyed all that my hands had done and what I had toiled to achieve, everything was meaningless, a chasing after the wind; nothing was gained under the sun.[76]

And with that account, the one person in history who achieved his worldly ambitions more

---

[76] Ecclesiastes 2:1-11.

completely than any other answered the question, "Then what?" His conclusion: "Nothing." Nothing under the sun can satisfy us completely. Everything you're striving for on earth eventually will disappoint, break down, give out, fail to meet expectations or die. Nothing under the sun will quench your thirst forever.

Quenching Your Thirst Forever

The good news is that King Solomon concluded his report on a hopeful note. While nothing under the sun can satisfy us completely, one who lives over the sun can do the trick. In Solomon's words: "Now all has been heard; here is the conclusion of the matter. Fear God and keep his commandments, for this is the whole duty of man."[77]

In other words, we need to set our sights a bit higher. The answer to the riddle of satisfaction doesn't come from the things of the earth. It comes from the God of the Universe. Just ask the woman at the well.

When the woman came to the well that day, she had planned to quench her thirst. She didn't realize that her soul was drier than her throat. That nothing of the world had given her lasting peace. And then something amazing happened. Jesus—God in the flesh—showed up.

---

[77] Ecclesiastes 12:13.

And he didn't just show up, he offered her living water: "Everyone who drinks this water will be thirsty again, but whoever drinks the water I give him will never thirst. Indeed, the water I give him will become in him a spring of water, welling up to eternal life."[78]

What is this living water that quenches our thirst forever? It is faith in Jesus Christ as our Savior.

When the disciples arrived at the well, they offered Jesus food. But somehow he wasn't hungry. "I have food to eat that you know nothing about," Jesus said. The disciples probably figured that Jesus had already grabbed lunch. Maybe hit a drive-thru in Samaria. Jesus set them straight: "My food . . . is to do the will of him who sent me and to finish his work."[79]

What is this food that satisfies our hunger forever? It is obeying God.

Whether we know it or not, each of us has a deep spiritual thirst which transcends even our greatest physical needs. And we've all tried to quench it with physical things. But nothing on earth can do it. No matter how hard we try, physical things can't satisfy spiritual needs.

But God can.

---

[78] John 4:13-14.
[79] John 4:31-35.

More than anything, God wants a relationship with us. Yet, because of our sinful nature, we can't have a relationship with a holy God. So God sent his only son, Jesus Christ, to die for our sins, yours and mine. By Christ's death on the cross, we are reconciled to God. For eternity. Welling up to eternal life. You need only believe and follow him.

To quench your thirst forever, you must have faith in Jesus Christ.

To satisfy our hunger forever, you must obey God.

Faith and obedience—spiritual food and drink for our thirsty, hungry souls.

What If?

It's not that money, possessions and fame are bad. Or that relationships, education, work, hobbies and experiences are meaningless. It's that they must be grounded in God to have real significance.

Jesus said "apart from me you can do nothing."[80] At least nothing that lasts forever. If you want your efforts to have eternal significance, they must be grounded in God. There's no other way.

---

[80] John 15:5.

Just as the question "Then what?" uncovers the emptiness of worldly endeavors, another question suggests the possibilities that lie in spiritual pursuits:

"What if?"

What if everything you did was designed to glorify God? What would your life look like?

Here's a picture:

Your mission is to glorify God, and everything you do revolves around him. You obey his commandments and strive to be like his son Jesus Christ. And you share Christ with everyone, mostly with your behavior, but also with your words. When you go to work, you earn money not just to support yourself and your family, but also to support ministry. Before spending money, you ask how the purchase honors God. Your ethics and behavior are different enough to make people curious about what makes you tick. You get together with friends to talk about serving others. When you eat, when you sleep, when you exercise, you are strengthening your body to do God's work. When you enjoy recreation and hobbies, you are renewing yourself to be an effective emissary of Christ. You raise your kids not just to be "good" people, but to be God's people. Everything you do, you do for God. Everything is an act of worship.

What if all of your efforts, all of your striving, had eternal significance?

What if you were never thirsty or hungry again?

It's Not About the Bike

1/25/10

Cam,

I know, it's the title of Lance Armstrong's first book. It also sums up our experience last weekend.

It all started when I decided to upgrade your entry level Trek mountain bike. Mom had a nice Jamis full-suspension mountain bike that she rode once before I crashed it into the garage, having forgotten it was sitting on the bike rack atop my SUV. The front fork was ruined, but the rest of the bike seemed intact. So I took both the Trek and the Jamis to the bike shop to have them build one bike with the best parts from each. It seemed like a success until we got home and noticed a huge crack right through the steering tube in the Jamis. The bike was useless, and I was out $127 for the work. I was incensed.

I marched into the bike shop the following morning with you in tow. I tried to explain the situation in a calm, logical manner, but the mechanics weren't having it. "Look," I said, "you cracked the frame yourself, or, at best, you failed to notice the crack. Either way, I'm out $127!" Well, things got a bit heated, and I said something I later regretted. "You guys might fix bikes for a living, but I'm a lawyer. I sue people for a living!"

My comment wasn't well received (except by you—you though it was hilarious!). The situation devolved into a shouting match. For a while, things went from bad to worse, but eventually everyone composed themselves. I apologized. Then we got down to business.

I ended up giving you my ten-year-old Specialized Stumpjumper, and I bought a brand new, 2009 Stumpjumper for myself. They must have felt bad about the whole situation because they gave me such a great deal on the new bike.

We went for a ride later that day at Quiet Waters Park, and I fell in love with my new bike. It rode like a carbon fiber dream. It wasn't until the next day when I did some internet research that I realized that Specialized had completely changed the Stumpjumer design in 2010 (which had been on the market several months by then). Not just style changes, but just about everything from stem to stern. No wonder I got such a good deal.

My love affair with my new bike lasted exactly 24 hours. As soon as I saw the 2010 model, I became dissatisfied with what I had.

I've been thinking there's a lesson here, and it's not about the bike. Had I bought a 2010 model, it too would have become obsolete. Maybe not immediately, but eventually. That's the way it is with possessions. There's always a better model next year.

When will I ever learn? Things will never satisfy me. Only God satisfies.

Dad

Pursue God

One day, Cameron, as hard as it is for me to say this, you will die. Just as I will. Just as everyone who has ever lived. On your death bed, you will not wish you had more stuff. Or more money. Or more knowledge. Or more food. Or more sex. Or more fun.

On your death bed, you'll be hoping that your light isn't going out permanently. That there's something on the other side. And you'll be wondering if your life mattered. If your efforts on earth had lasting significance.

Worldly pursuits will never satisfy you completely. Only Godly pursuits can do that. Only God can quench your thirst forever. C.S. Lewis had it right when he said "aim at heaven, and you will get earth thrown in; aim at earth, and you will get neither."

Don't aim at earth, Cameron. Don't even aim for the stars; aim above them. Aim for the God of the Universe.

If you're ready to aim that high, then you'll need to get ready for your great work.

Lesson Eight

You Were Destined for Greatness

"Be a hero."

—Lillie Silverglate (my grandmother)

You Just Have to Wait

The elevator arrived on the 24th floor of the downtown Miami skyscraper. I hopped in and pressed "L" for lobby.

At the first stop on the 22nd floor, a young man dressed in a pinstripe suit walked in. He had a leather briefcase in one hand and legal files in the other. From the looks of it, he was a brand new lawyer.

On the 20th floor, a distinguished older gentleman, also clad in lawyerly attire, boarded the elevator.

The two recognized each other and exchanged pleasantries. Then the subject turned to work.

"I don't know about this lawyer stuff," the young man remarked candidly.

The comment caught me off guard, and I found myself listening in on their conversation.

"I know what you mean, but you just have to wait," the older lawyer counseled.

"Wait?" the young lawyer asked in a hopeful tone. "Wait for what?"

I was now listening intently and relieved that he asked the question. If he didn't, I would have. The old sage was about to enlighten his young colleague with his years of wisdom and experience. I leaned in so as not to miss a word.

"I don't know. You just have to wait," the older lawyer responded.

With that, the elevator arrived at the lobby, and the two men went their separate ways.

I just stood there, dumbfounded. "You just have to wait?" Are you kidding me? That was all the wisdom he could muster?

Here were two educated guys. Both seemingly discontent. Both waiting for something to change. Neither doing anything to effect change.

As it turns out, they're not alone. Most of us seem to be waiting.

What are You Waiting For?

The last words my Grandma Lillie said to me weren't "be careful," or "don't get hurt" or "take care of yourself." Any of those things would have made sense for an elderly woman who buried two husbands, four sons and a granddaughter. She was an immigrant who beat cancer, beat the odds and established herself as the beloved matriarch of a large, unwieldy family.

But that's not what she said. Her last words to me were, "Be a hero." I was 19 at the time, and that's exactly what I wanted to be.

I guess it's what every boy wants—to be a hero. We start off with so much hope and enthusiasm, ready to change the world. Ready to invent something or cure cancer. Ready to save people from evil villains or burning buildings. Ready to make a difference.

And then life happens.

Our dreams are whittled away until, eventually, we give up on them altogether. We trade ideals for reality. Passion for comfort. Adventure for safety. Our dreams give way to getting by and paying the mortgage. I imagine that's what Thoreau was thinking when he wrote, "Most men live lives of quiet desperation and go to the grave with the song still in them."[81]

There's an epidemic out there of low-grade discontentment. Why? Because the hero inside us is alive. He may be buried, but he still has a pulse. And he nags, and he prods and he nudges. He grabs hold of our soul and won't let go. Deep down, we still want to be heroes. It's what those two lawyers in the elevator wanted, even if they couldn't articulate it. It's what we all want.

It's what you want.

Yet we never seem to do anything about it. We just wait for something to change. We wait and we endure.

In fact, you might be waiting right now.

Well, what if I told you that your wait is over? What if I told you that greatness is within your grasp? What if I told you that I know the way to get there?

Arrogant as it may sound, I believe I've stumbled on the secret. The very secret to greatness.

---

[81] Henry David Thoreau, *Walden* (Boston: Ticknor & Fields 1854).

And it's time to share it with you, Cameron. Indeed, it is your destiny.

THE SECRET TO GREATNESS

She was just being a mom. Like any mom, she wanted the best for her sons.

So the mother of two of the disciples approached Jesus. She had a favor to ask. Nothing big, really. Just a little request.

"Grant that one of these two sons of mine may sit at your right and the other at your left in your kingdom," she petitioned.[82]

That's all. She just wanted her two boys to be the most important men in the universe. What mother wouldn't?

But Jesus did what he does best. He rocked her world. He turned things right on their head.

He said "whoever wants to be great among you must be your servant, and whoever wants to be first will be your slave—just as the Son of Man did not come to be served, but to serve, and to give his life as a ransom for many."[83]

---

[82] Matthew 20:21.
[83] Matthew 20:26-28.

You see greatness on God's scorecard is measured not by power or money or influence. Greatness is measured by service.

That is the secret to greatness. To be great, you must be a servant.

There is no other way.

You Were Made to Serve

If service is the secret to greatness, why are we so miserable? I believe the answer is that we primarily serve ourselves. And self-seeking always leaves us empty.

As a young lawyer, I read Dale Carnegie's self-help books. After all, I wanted to "win friends and influence people" as much as the next guy. But the more I read, the more disappointed I became. The suggestion in all of his books was to think about others more than ourselves. In fact, he dedicated an entire book to *How to Stop Worrying and Start Living*.[84] The book can be summarized in one simple phrase: "Worry about someone else's problems."

As a young man, that sounded hokey to me. But I've learned that he was exactly right. I spend a fair amount of time serving only myself, and it

---

[84] Dale Carnegie, *How to Stop Worrying and Start Living* (New York: Simon & Schuster, 1985), 175.

always leaves me empty. My universe is small and confining when I'm at the center of it.

An over-used analogy is the Sea of Galilee, the body of water upon which Jesus walked. It is vibrant and teeming with life. The Galilee receives water upstream from the Jordan River and sends it downstream to the Dead Sea. It always gives away what flows into it. The Dead Sea, in contrast, only receives water. It gives nothing. As a result, it is stagnant and devoid of life.

That pretty well sums up the human condition. When we only receive and don't give, we become stagnant, putrid, dead.

Oh, but when we give, we're alive. That's because we were made to give and to serve. It is knit right into our DNA.

I like to receive more than most, but I can scarcely remember the gifts I have gotten over the years. However, I can remember every significant gift I have ever given. I'll bet you can too. What we give has infinitely more impact on us than what we get.

Whenever I have stepped out of my comfort zone to serve others, I have always come away enriched by the process. When we give and when we serve, we are blessed in return. Not necessarily by the people we serve, but by God.

German philosopher Albert Schweitzer described it this way: "I don't know what your destiny will be, but one thing I do know: the only ones among you who will be really happy are those who have sought and found how to serve."

Chinese philosopher Confucius said it like this: "He who wishes to secure the good of others has already secured his own."

American philosopher Ralph Waldo Emerson offered this explanation: "It is one of the most beautiful compensations of life, that no man can sincerely try to help another without helping himself."

These were some smart guys, each of whom glimpsed the truth about service. But there is one even greater. One who is truth incarnate. And he said it first: "Give, and it will be given to you. A good measure, pressed down, shaken together and running over, will be poured into your lap. For with the measure you use, it will be measured to you."[85]

That's God's economy. It's the law of opposites. If you want to be great, if you want to be truly blessed, you must serve others.

---

[85] Luke 6:38.

What Does it Mean to be a Servant?

In God's view, the only way to be a hero is to be a servant. And the only way to be a servant is (you guessed it) to serve. In fact, Jesus declares throughout the gospels that how much we serve others reflects how much we love God.[86] Service is an indispensable part of the equation.

But what does it mean to be a servant?

The entire focus of our lives must be about others. Instead of being self-centered, we must be other-centered. Not just during the occasional mission trip or volunteer project. Always. That's what heroes do. They focus on others, not just in spurts and not just when it's convenient. They do it all the time. They always place others before themselves. That's what makes them great.

The other hallmark of a servant is his goal—to further God's kingdom. Service for service sake is okay, but it's not enough. Whether you give a man a fish or teach him to fish, eventually, the man will die. The only question is where he will be spending eternity.

That's why helping people with their physical needs always must be a gateway to satisfying their spiritual needs. Physical needs are temporary; spiritual needs are eternal.

---

[86] See, e.g., Matthew 10:42, John 21:15-17.

Jesus fed the masses, healed the sick and raised the dead as a means to spread his Gospel message. It is, after all, difficult to receive spiritual guidance when you're hungry, sick or dead. However, all of the people whom Jesus fed, healed and resurrected eventually died. Jesus' mission was not to end hunger, or illness or suffering, but to conquer sin, thereby restoring man's relationship with God.

This must be our mission as well. Feed the hungry. Help the sick. Defend the defenseless. But do it as an emissary of Jesus Christ, spreading his gospel message with every act of service. Remember Jesus' admonition: [A]part from me you can do nothing."[87] If our good works do not involve Christ, they will not have eternal significance.

That's what it means to be a hero—to make Godly service our core mission on earth. If you stay true to this quest, God will use you in ways you can hardly imagine. In fact, I believe he will give you a great work.

I am Doing a Great Work and I Cannot Come Down

Jerusalem was in need of a great work. The Persians destroyed the Holy City in 586 B.C, including the most sacred site in all of Judaism—the

---

[87] John 15:5.

Temple that King Solomon built.[88] Eventually, the Temple was rebuilt, but the city walls remained in ruins. In those days, a city relied on its walls for protection. Without walls, there was no city.

Nehemiah was the cupbearer to the Persian King Artaxerxes. A Jew, Nehemiah was aggrieved that the walls of his homeland lay in ruins. After a period of prayer and fasting, Nehemiah felt a calling from God. He approached King Artaxerxes, the most powerful man in the land, and asked for permission to return to Jerusalem to rebuild its walls. This project would have been difficult for anyone, but for Nehemiah, it should have been impossible. He wasn't an architect or a general contractor or even a subcontractor. He was a cupbearer—he fetched wine for the king. And to make matters worse, he had no tools or building materials.

But God provided.

Not only did the king grant Nehemiah's outrageous request, he provided him transportation and building materials. When Nehemiah arrived in Jerusalem, he organized the people into groups and assigned them specific sections of the wall. And the project commenced. The downtrodden and desperate Jews were now filled with purpose as they worked shoulder-to-shoulder toward their impossible dream.

---

[88] The Book of Nehemiah.

Like every great story though, there were villains. The main one was Sanballat, the Governor of Samaria. A rebuilt city was a direct threat to Sanballat's authority, so he desperately wanted the project to fail. He tried threats, ridicule, treachery and sabotage. The rebuilding project became so dangerous that half the men were assigned to work and the other half to guard the workers. Those who carried the building materials did their work with one hand and carried their weapon in the other.

All of Sanballat's attempts to derail the project ultimately failed. And eventually, miraculously, the "impossible" project neared completion.

But Sanballat had one last trick up his sleeve. He sent a messenger to invite Nehemiah to a meeting, really an ambush. In fact, the messenger approached Nehemiah not once, but four times. And each time, Nehemiah gave him the same reply:

"I am doing a great work and I cannot come down."[89]

Nehemiah never did come down, and the impossible project was completed in a miraculous 52 days. Had Nehemiah remained in his comfortable, safe position bringing wine to the king, he would have died anonymously and unfulfilled. As Thoreau lamented, "with the song

---

[89] Nehemiah 6:3 (NASB).

still in him." But he took a chance. He answered God's call. He dared to be great. And 2,500 years later, we're still talking about him.

From Jerusalem to Haiti

I was tapped earlier this year to go to Haiti on my first mission trip. Our guide was Haitian-American Pastor Joanem Floreal. I didn't know Pastor Floreal prior to the trip. I learned that as a young man, he left Haiti for the United States where he became a Methodist pastor. But his homeland remained in his heart.

Pastor Floreal is a modern day Nehemiah. The only difference is that the land of his forefathers isn't in the Middle East; it's on a small island in the Caribbean. Haiti is the most densely populated country in the western hemisphere. It is racked by poverty, disease, deforestation and corruption. In 2008, the island was ravaged by three powerful hurricanes.[90] To many observers, the situation seems hopeless.

But Pastor Floreal is not an observer. He's a warrior. He is a mighty servant of God.

When we landed in Cap Haitian, we were met by hordes of beggars, many of them children.

---

[90] A year after our trip to Haiti, the island was rocked by a cataclysmic earthquake that killed over 200,000 inhabitants. Pastor Floreal is still building, undeterred by the "set back."

Pastor Floreal practically incited a riot when he began handing out money. We had to jump into our car for safety. I'll never forget the look on the faces of the kids as we sped off. It was a look of sheer hopelessness.

Our group was somber that evening. Quite a contrast to the next day, when we traveled to a little village where Pastor Floreal has started a school. The building was a work in progress. Two stories of raw cinder block. No windows or doors. No roof. No bathrooms. But that little, ramshackle school accommodated over a hundred kids. And they were happy. They were singing and laughing. They had hope.

I was struck by the contrast between the kids who were begging at the airport and their counterparts at Pastor Floreal's school. One group was desperate, the other hopeful. Why the difference? It was one man. One great man with a heroic vision.

In my book (literally), Pastor Floreal is a rock star. Like Nehemiah, God placed in his heart a holy burden for his homeland. God gave him a vision, and he answered the call. Where others saw poverty, he saw potential. Where others saw problems, he saw possibilities. Where others saw devastation, he saw hope.

I want to be like Pastor Floreal. He is doing a great work. I hope he never comes down.

You Were Made to do a Great Work

My son, at some point in your life, you will be called to do a great work. You'll know it by these attributes:

1. It will start with a passion or a burden that God has placed in your heart. Our passions and burdens are not accidental. God uses them to stimulate action.

2. It will involve other people. Great works are never solitary endeavors. They are meant to be accomplished as part of a team, and the goal must be directed toward serving others.

3. It will advance God's purposes. The work must be of God, not man. That's what makes it great.

4. It will be too great to do without God. Even the most qualified team will not be able to accomplish the great work without God's assistance. If the team can get the job done without supernatural involvement, the job isn't big enough.

5. God will provide the means to accomplish it. Where God guides, he provides. If the work is of God, he'll provide the tools to get it done.

While you're waiting for your great work, Cameron, I hope you won't be sitting around. I hope you will dedicate yourself every day to serving others. Service which advances God's kingdom. Service which is anchored in Christ.

My Great Work

In my very first journal entry, I wrote: "How many people who are really succeeding in the world give it up to pursue a higher purpose? I'd like to believe that if and when that purpose is ever made clear to me, your father would be such a person."

Well, it took me quite a while, but I finally realized my higher purpose. My great work. When you were just seven months old, I wrote you this letter:

10/10/95

Cam,

I'm on a plane flying home from Philadelphia. Window seat. Autumn day. Blue sky. White, puffy clouds.

It was a business trip. A deposition in a medical malpractice case. You're only seven months old, so you don't understand this. But someday you will (probably at eight months).

The reason for my letter is that I feel overcome with a great sense of purpose. Maybe it's because I'm gliding through the air at 30,000 feet. But at this moment, I feel perfect clarity. I see the very reason for my existence.

It is you, Cameron.

You are the reason I'm here. I was made to be your dad.

I don't know what possessed me to write this. I hope it does not portend a crash. But if it does, I hope somehow you recover this letter and remember me by it.

I love you forever.

Dad

P.S. The deposition went well.

My great passion in life, Cameron, is being your father. To raise you as a man of God. A man who will serve others.

Raising a child is a team effort. In fact, I believe the primary reason God put your mother and me together was to raise you. And we need all the help we can get. Why? Because life is a masterpiece involving many artists: Pastors, teachers, coaches, friends, youth groups and all of the other positive influences available. Even more, we need God to guide our efforts and provide the means to accomplish our goal.

When you were an infant, I went on a law firm retreat. One of the speakers said that success requires sacrifice. Working on nights and weekend. Time away from our families. He suggested that the sacrifice would be worth it because the goal was so important—success.

I wondered whether you would benefit more by a successful father or one who was home on nights and weekends. I made a promise to myself right then and there. I vowed that I would always place my home life ahead of my work life. And that I would give everything I had to being the best father and husband I could be. I figured the only ones for whom I needed to be a hero were you and mom.

When we're dead and gone, others usually sum up our lives in one short sentence. "He was a good lawyer." "He had a good sense of humor." "He was smart." "He was a jerk." Whether we like it or not, our lives are boiled down to a sound bite.

When I'm gone, I hope they say one thing. That I was a good husband and a good dad. That'll be enough for me.

In my own way, I'm doing a great work. And I can assure you, I will not come down.

BE A HERO

That's the lesson on greatness, Cameron. When you accepted Christ as your savior, you were born into nobility. In your veins flows the royal blood of the King of kings and Lord of lords. When you made that one auspicious decision, you became destined for greatness.

So under the authority vested in me as your earthly father, and in the immortal words of your great grandmother, I hereby commission you:

Be a hero!

Don't live a life of comfort and complacency. Don't sit around waiting for something to change. Make it happen. Step out of your comfort zone. Dare to be great.

But to be great, you must be a servant. There is no other way.

Now that you're on your way to greatness, Cameron, I will tell you about the greatest thing in the world. I will tell you about love.

Lesson Nine

You Were Born to Love

"Falling in love requires a pulse. Staying in love requires a plan."

—Andy Stanley

Finding Ms. Right

Well Cameron, I contemplated writing this lesson about how to find your future wife. After all, it's inevitable. One day you'll meet a girl and fall in love. But how will you know if she's the one with whom you were meant to spend the rest of your life? Then it occurred to me that if you're not sure, she's probably not the one.

When you meet your soul-mate, you'll know it. There won't be any ambiguity. The bigger question is whether you can stay in love forever. To do that, you'll need more than passion. You'll need a plan.

The Wonder of New Love

Harps played. Angels sang. Fireworks exploded.

Everything changed that autumn evening on September 11, 1982. It was a frat party at the University of Florida. I was 19, and all things were possible.

Her name was Kathy Clark. She was a "little sister" of my fraternity. She was popular and beautiful . . . and way out of my league. I was sure she'd have no interest in a poor, insecure, Jewish kid from Miami. But what if? What if she'd just dance with me? Well, my son, fate is a funny thing. A cynic might chalk it up to raging teenage hormones. Or large quantities of beer. Or the DJ blasting Journey's "Don't Stop Believin'." But somehow I mustered the nerve to ask her to dance.

Well, not exactly to dance. I could only summon enough courage to ask her to *reserve* a dance for me (a ritual practiced in the Deep South before the Civil War). Asking this ravishing beauty to engage in the physical act of dancing seemed way too risky. After all, a request to dance could be rejected on any number of grounds, but a request to *reserve* a dance could not, in good faith, be denied.

Amazingly, my plan worked. Kat had no choice but to say "yes" to my lame effort at courtship. The problem was I couldn't get beyond the conquered territory of asking her to reserve dances. By the time midnight rolled around, Kat must have reserved half-a-dozen dances for me. So when I asked her to reserve lucky number seven, she said "no."

"Excuse me?" I asked innocently.

"No, I will not reserve another dance for you," she responded.

"Why not?" I inquired.

"Because I think you're a snob."

"A snob? How could you say such a thing?"

"Because you keep asking me to reserve a dance, but then you never dance with me."

I must have been so stunned by the comment that I temporarily forgot my fear. The gauntlet had been laid down. A challenge had been issued. In what seemed like slow motion, I looked my future wife right in the eyes, cleared my throat, extended my hand and said, "L…e…t'…s……d…a…n…c…e."

Kat took my hand. And we danced. We danced all night. And we've been dancing together ever since.

Then Reality Sets In

The first few months of our relationship were heavenly. The sky seemed bluer; the grass, greener. Food even tasted better. Everything was right in the world.

Like every new couple, we put our best foot forward. Kat cooked for me. I wrote her poetry. She laughed at my jokes. I took her out on dates. She introduced me to her friends. I pretended to like them.

Whatever faults we had were overlooked. The only thing in the world that mattered was each other.

But it's inevitable. The infatuation period eventually ends and reality sets in. So it is with every relationship and ours was no different. Gradually, we remove our masks and reveal the broken person underneath. The one with faults. The one with needs. The one who is self-seeking.

And then something really strange happens.

At some point in most intimate relationships, an unwelcome visitor creeps in—competition. It's a competition to be right. When conflict inevitably arrives, we want to prove that we are right and our spouse is wrong—as if we could ever know such a thing. Being right becomes all important. It becomes important enough to fight about. It even becomes more important than the relationship itself. And like any competition, score is kept, records are never purged, and the combatants are occasionally injured. But in this competition, there are no winners.

The statistics are grim. Half of all marriages end in divorce. And many of those that don't aren't exactly thriving. The situation doesn't improve with age either. Think about it. When was the last time you saw a married couple over 60 who were head-over-heels in love? I've seen older couples in restaurants who don't say a word to each other the entire meal. Have they already said everything they have to say to their spouse?

It's a sobering question, but are we all doomed to fall out of love? Is it even possible for a couple to fall in love and stay in love forever? Not just endure the relationship, but thrive in it?

Is there such a thing as true love?

I believe there is, but it's exceedingly rare. And that's sad because true love is exactly what God intended for us.

True Love

The Scriptures give us a vivid description of true love. A love that is attainable by human beings with the help of God. It is a description that has never been equaled by any author, singer or poet. It is a description inspired by God Himself.

> Love is patient, love is kind. It does not envy, it does not boast, it is not proud. It is not self-seeking, it is not easily angered, it keeps no record of wrongs. Love does not delight in evil but rejoices in truth. It always protects, always trusts, always hopes, always perseveres. Love never fails.
>
> * * *
>
> And now three things remain: faith, hope and love. But the greatest of these is love.[91]

Yes, true love exists. The Scriptures bear witness to it. Still, our own experience tells us otherwise.

So just how do we find this true love?

LOVE IS A VERB

Jesus Christ answered the age-old riddle of true love. He answered it once and for all in a groundbreaking, breathtaking, seven-word sentence. In fact, he described it not as a suggestion but a commandment:

> "This is my command: Love each other."[92]

---

[91] 1 Corinthians 13:4-13.
[92] John 15:17.

If you weren't reading carefully, you might have missed it. Jesus uses the word "love" not as a noun, but a verb. He describes love not as a thing, but an action. He's not suggesting that we find love; he's commanding us to engage in love. Nowhere does his commandment suggest that love is a feeling that we can fall into or out of. Nor does it say that love is contingent on who we marry or whether we're being treated fairly.

The commandment is a simple, no-nonsense call to action: "Love each other." It's the secret of true love. Love is a verb.

Author Stephen Covey clearly understood this concept when he described his conversation with a man seeking marital advice:

> "My wife and I just don't have the same feelings for each other we used to have. I guess I just don't love her anymore and she doesn't love me. What can I do?"
>
> "The feeling isn't there anymore?" I asked.
>
> "That's right," he reaffirmed. "And we have three children we're really concerned about. What do you suggest?"
>
> "Love her," I replied.

"I told you, the feeling just isn't there anymore."

"Love her."

"You don't understand. The feeling of love just isn't there."

"Then love her. If the feeling isn't there, that's a good reason to love her."

"But how do you love when you don't love?"

"My friend, love is a verb. Love—the feeling—is a fruit of love the verb. So love her. Serve her. Sacrifice. Listen to her. Empathize. Appreciate. Affirm her. Are you willing to do that?"[93]

As the dialogue shows, the only person in the world we can control is our self. I cannot make my wife love me, but I can love her. I can sacrifice for her. I can engage in loving actions toward her. And when I do, something magical happens. Her feelings of love for me grow. Not only that, my feelings of love for her grow. Not just because I'm getting love, but because I'm giving it. Why? For the same reason that parents

---

[93] Stephen R. Covey, *The 7 Habits of Highly Effective People* (New York: Simon & Schuster, Inc. 1989), 79-80.

have such strong feelings of love for their children. We make a huge investment in our kids by sacrificing so greatly for them. We tend to love what we invest in, and we tend to be careless where we haven't invested. Marriage is worth the investment.

Here's the unassailable truth: Loving feelings follow loving efforts. Love the noun is the fruit of love the verb. This is the miraculous snowball effect when one person loves sacrificially.

You Can be Right Or You Can be in Relationship

The Bible describes the relationship between husband and wife as one of submission and sacrifice. Wives are to submit to their husbands, and husbands are to love their wives as Christ loved the church. [94] How did Christ love the church? Sacrificially. The all-powerful Son of God allowed himself to be turned over to the authorities, before whom he offered no defense. Even though he was innocent, even though he could have played the "God card" and changed the outcome in an instant, Jesus allowed himself to be tried, convicted and crucified—for us.

Even though he was right, Jesus opted for relationship. And because of his sacrifice—to

---

[94] Ephesians 5:22-33.

the point of death—all mankind is able to have a relationship with God.

That's how husbands and wives are to love each other. Through submission and sacrifice. It's what's involved in every successful marriage. The husband and wife love each other even when they're offended, even when they've been wronged and even when they're not loved in return. And most importantly, they don't compete against each other. They subordinate the urge to be right for the greater good of the relationship. They sacrifice the "me" for the "we."

As Pastor Andy Stanley says, "You can't have it both ways. You can either be right, or you can be in relationship." As with many of the great truths in life, I had to discover this one the hard way . . .

Love Hurts

Every couple has their first fight, and Kat and I were no different.

We were several months into our relationship when I caught her in a lie. It was something trivial. In fact, I can't even recall what it was about. All I remember is I had her dead to rites, and the future lawyer in me couldn't leave it alone. She had to be brought to justice, and I was just the man to do it.

She didn't deny it when I confronted her. But she didn't admit it either. She chose a third option, the one an animal chooses when it senses danger. She fled—literally. Humiliated by my direct, in-your-face confrontation over her lie, Kat took off running through the University of Florida campus. Not being one to resist a challenge, I gave chase.

In one building she ran, and in I followed. Then out of the building she ran, and out I followed. The whole time, I yelled after her, "Admit it, you lied!" I don't know how many buildings our game of cat and mouse took us through, but we eventually ended up in the main library—a huge gothic building that served as the University's first law school back in the day. I was gaining ground as we raced up the stairwell when I caught a glimpse of the door closing on the third floor. I exited into the cavernous main room of the library. My eyes scanned the rows of tables filled with engrossed students.

But no Kat.

Like a lion stalking its prey, I tip-toed into the stacks of dusty old books. And there, in the corner of the room, crouching between Salinger and Shakespeare, I spotted her. She was trapped. Nowhere else to run. Nowhere else to hide.

She'd finally have to admit that I was right—she lied.

I snuck up from behind and tapped her ever so gently on the shoulder. Startled, she wheeled around in one fluid motion and slapped me right across the face! I just stood there in stunned disbelief as the sound echoed throughout the room. Every eye in the library must have been on me. But I didn't notice. All I could see was the wild-eyed look of panic on Kat's face as tears ran down her cheeks.

Suddenly, I didn't care about being right anymore. I did the only thing I could do. I threw my arms around her, and I loved her. It's the only time in my life that I literally turned the other cheek.

As my friend Eric Stewart is fond of saying, being right is a dangerous place to be in an argument with your wife. I know what he means.

The Greatest Thing in the World

One of my favorite movies is The Princess Bride.[95] It is a story of true love, and it sums up the lesson of submission and sacrifice.

The story begins with a beautiful young woman named Buttercup who lives on a farm in the fictional country of Florin. She delights in ordering the

---

[95] *The Princess Bride*, written by William Goldman, directed by Rob Reiner (20th Century Fox 1987).

farm-hand Westley to perform chores. Westley's only response is, "As you wish."

Buttercup: "Farm Boy, fetch me this."

Westley: "As you wish."

Buttercup: "Farm Boy, get me that."

Westley: "As you wish."

Buttecup: "Farm Boy, polish my saddle."

Westley: "As you wish."

Eventually, Buttercup realizes a profound truth. When Westley says "As you wish," what he really means is "I love you." And then she realizes something equally profound. She loves him too.

The two pledge their undying love for each other. But Westley must venture out on his own to find his fortune so the two can marry. Buttercup is worried he'll never return.

Buttercup: "What if something happens to you?"

Westley: "Hear this now, I will always come for you."

Buttercup: "But how can you be so sure?"

Westley: "This is true love. You think this happens every day?"

Westley's adventure begins, but along the journey, the unthinkable happens. He is killed. Desperate, his friends Fezzik and Inigo Montoya take his body to the local magician, Miracle Max (played by Billy Crystal). As it turns out, Westley is only "mostly dead." But Max is hesitant to help, uncertain about the justness of their cause. So Max pumps Westley's lungs with air and listens for his explanation.

Max: What's so important? What you got here that's worth living for?

Westley: "T . . . r . . . ue . . . love."

Inigo Montoya: "True love. You heard him. You could not ask for a more noble cause than that."

Max: "Sonny, true love is the greatest thing in the world. Except for a nice MLT—mutton lettuce and tomato sandwich, where the mutton is nice and lean and the tomato is ripe. They're so perky, I love that."

The story had it right—true love is a noble cause. It's worth living and dying for. It's worth fighting for. It's even worth submitting and sacrificing for.

True love really is the greatest thing in the world.

Forever Yours

But that's just Hollywood. You still may be wondering if real people can fall in love and stay in love forever. I can tell you without a doubt that it is possible. I know because my parents did it.

My dad wasn't much for lectures. He was a man not of words, but of action. Like the quote says, "He didn't tell me how to live; he lived and let me watch him do it."[96] The same is true for my mom. My parents didn't so much tell us how to live as show us. And one of things they showed us was what a marriage is supposed to look like. They loved each other like they loved their children—sacrificially.

I once heard someone say that to be a good father, you need to have good mothering instincts. As odd as it sounds, my father was a good mother. He was a big, strong guy, but he never hid his emotions. He would yell, laugh and cry with equal intensity. He was also a good cook, a shameless advocate for his kids and a wonderful caregiver. One of his endearing quirks was his belief that rubbing alcohol could cure just about every illness. When one of his kids got a headache, he would tie an alcohol-soaked handkerchief around our head. It had absolutely no therapeutic benefit, but the sting of the

---

[96] Clarence Budington Keller.

alcohol dripping in our eyes always made us forget the headache.

I can see why my mom fell in love with him. She remained single until she was 39, as if she'd been waiting for my dad her whole life—even though they'd never met.

Their first date was classic. My mom was staying at her brother's house, and her niece spiked a fever. Others were at home who could have taken care of the little girl, but my mom thought it would be irresponsible to leave her. The date would have to be canceled. My dad, a widower who raised two kids of his own, arrived to pick up my mom and was apprised of the situation. He knew just what to do. He rolled up his sleeves, marched up the stairs to the patient's room and treated her with, what else, rubbing alcohol. Miraculously, her fever broke! He rolled down his sleeves, turned to my mom and said, "Let's go, Gertrude!" And off they went. Not to a romantic restaurant. Or to a show. Or to a nightclub.

On their first date, my dad took my mom home to meet his mother. And within two weeks, they were engaged to be married.

My dad was a good mother.

And my mother, well, she was a great mother.

Times were good when I was little. Dad had a terrific job, and mom stayed home with the kids. They were both in relatively good health. But then my dad had a heart attack and had to retire. Money got tight and my dad got sick, real sick—triple bypass surgery, diabetes, leg amputation. My mother loved and cared for him through it all. Tenderly and lovingly, she nursed her husband back to health.

Then my mom got sick—cancer—but she wasn't as fortunate. My dad tried to nurse her back to health, but it wasn't to be. At the young age of 57, my mom succumbed to her illness.

Even though I was only 14 at the time, I remember my last conversation with my mother like it was yesterday. I was at her bedside at the hospital, just the two of us. She was hooked up to an oxygen tank; she could barely breathe. She was lapsing in and out of consciousness. During a lucid moment, she whispered what would be her last words to me. She said, "Take care of your father." That was it. Not, "I love you son," or "I'm proud of you," or "I'll always be in your heart." No, as the life was ebbing out of her body, she was thinking of her husband. She wanted me to take care of her husband. That's how much she loved the man.

That's true love. It's sacrificial love.

When my mom died the following day, my father's spirit died too. He never recovered. He lived a broken man for a few more years—long enough to see me off to college—before following his wife to the grave. When he died, I inherited his wedding band. I can't wear it because it's about five sizes too big for me. I can't cut it down either because it's inscribed with a Bible verse: "I am my beloved's and my beloved is mine."[97] My parents lived out that verse every day of their marriage, not in words but in actions.

Mario Cuomo once said, "I talk and I talk, and I haven't taught people in fifty years what my father taught me by example in one week." That's how I feel about my parents. One day I hope to grow into my father's wedding band.

I know that two people can fall in love and stay in love forever because I saw my parents do it. They loved each other through better and worse, in richer and poorer, in sickness and health. Only death could break the bonds of their love.

That's true love. It's love that lasts forever.

Don't Stop Believin'

So I come back to where it all began—a frat party at the University of Florida in the fall of 1982. I never imagined that the greatest thing I would

---

[97] Song of Solomon 2:16.

ever accomplish in life was asking Kathy Clark to dance with me when I was 19. But if I hadn't, there would be no you, Cameron. And the truth is, there wouldn't be a me either. At least, not the same me.

Marriage is the best finishing school there is. It refines you. It smoothes out the rough edges (some of them, anyway). It makes you better. It made me better. Marriage exists not just to make us happy, but to make us whole. My wife has made me whole.

Over the years, Kat has taught me many things. Not so much in words but in deeds. She has shown me patience and kindness. She has shown me faith and hope. But the greatest thing she has shown me is love. Because of Kat, I know unconditional, sacrificial love. I know true love.

Don't ever doubt true love, son. It's real. It exists. And it's worth living for. In fact, it's the only thing worth living for.

True love is the greatest thing in the world.

You Were Born to Love

Cameron, one day you will meet a girl, fall in love and marry. But the real question is whether you can stay in love forever. I'm here to tell you that you can do it, but you'll need a plan.

You will have to treat love as a verb. It's not about whom you marry or what she does or doesn't do. It's on you, son. The only person in the world you can control is yourself.

You will have to love your wife no matter what. Even if the feeling of love is not there. Even if she is not loving you in return. Even when you're right and she's wrong. Remember, you can't have it both ways. You can either be right or you can be in relationship.

Love your wife like Christ loved us. Elevate her needs above your own. Be patient. Be kind. Forgive her as many times as God has forgiven you.

Do not be proud or self-seeking. Do not be easily angered. Always assume the best in her, and keep no record of wrongs.

What's good for your wife is good for you because you are one flesh. So sacrifice for her. Empathize with her. Affirm her. Appreciate her. Listen to her. Cherish her. Know her heart. Fight for her. Die for her if necessary.

If you have to speak truth to her, do it in love.

And persevere. Always persevere.

If you engage in these actions of love, I promise you that the feeling of love will never be far behind.

Above all, keep God at the center of your marriage. The closer you and your wife become with God, the closer you will become with each other.

So I leave you with this simple charge, son: Love your wife.

It won't always be easy, but it's worth it. True love is worth it. It is the greatest thing in the world.

Now that you know about love, Cameron, you're ready for your final lesson. You're ready to begin the journey of your life.

LESSON TEN

LIFE IS A JOURNEY, NOT A DESTINATION

"EVERY DAY YOU MAKE PROGRESS. EVERY STEP MAY BE FRUITFUL. YET THERE WILL STRETCH OUT BEFORE YOU AN EVER-LENGTHENING, EVER-ASCENDING, EVER-IMPROVING PATH. YOU KNOW YOU WILL NEVER GET TO THE END OF THE JOURNEY. BUT THIS, SO FAR FROM DISCOURAGING, ONLY ADDS TO THE JOY AND GLORY OF THE CLIMB."

—WINSTON CHURCHILL

"THE REWARD IS THE JOURNEY."

—CHINESE PROVERB

ARE WE THERE YET?

It's the mantra of every kid who's ever sat in the back seat of a car during a road trip. "Are we there yet? Are we there yet? Are we there yet?"

And Cameron, you were no different. One trip in particular sticks in my mind. We were on vacation in Ireland, driving the Ring of Kerry—a 106 mile stretch of road along the country's Iveragh Peninsula. On it are some of the most spectacular views in the world—emerald hills, soaring cliffs, dizzying drop-offs, all set against the deep blue waters of the North Atlantic.

But at seven years old, you weren't impressed. All you wanted to know was "are we there yet?" How ironic, I thought to myself. As the name "*Ring* of Kerry" suggests, the path is one big circle. There is no "there" to get. You're "there" the whole time.

Isn't that just like life? We focus so much on the future and the past that we miss out on the present. We want to know when we're going to get "there," but we're "there" the whole time.

The Mad Dash to the Grave

In a few short years I'll be 50! How on earth did I get here?

In my heart, I'm still an invincible 21-year-old, bench pressing 300 pounds and eating raw eggs. In reality, I'm a creaky 47-year-old with bad knees and a high fiber diet. Just yesterday I was a young hotshot ready to set the world on fire. I blinked my eyes and I'm a bespectacled, middle-aged lawyer ready for a game of Scrabble.

How did I get here? The same way we all did. Much too quickly.

From the moment we're born, we're striving for the next step. How soon can we lift our head, respond to sound, smile, roll over, eat solid food, crawl, talk, walk, go in the potty, read, ride a bike.

What's the rush?

We love to engage in "when and then thinking." "When (<u>you fill in the blank</u>) happens, then I'll be happy." We never seem to get there though.

When we're little kids, we can't wait to start school. Then we'll be happy. But when we get there, we're already thinking about the next grade. The thing a kindergartener wants most in life is to be a first grader. Of course, that gets old too. Elementary students look forward to middle school, but soon can't wait to move on to high school. In high school we start dreaming of the independence of college. Then it's a job, marriage and kids. Then a better job. Eventually, we get older, and we pine for grandchildren. Then we want to retire to spend time with them and enjoy our hard-earned golden years.

But inevitably, we get sick. And we're put somewhere to die. That part we don't look forward to, but we sure seem to be rushing to get there.

We have friends who built an addition onto their house for the wife's terminally ill parents. The parents died sooner than expected, so they converted the addition into a pool room. I'm not saying I blame them, but it's a sobering thought. When you die, someone might just put a pool table where your bed used to be.

So why are we in such a rush to get there? We keep thinking that the next stage of life will make us happy, but we never quite get "there." If we could only slow down long enough, maybe we'd enjoy the journey. Maybe even learn something along the way.

A Tale of Two Journeys

Moses was a failure.

At least, in one sense—he never made it to his intended destination. He never made it to the Promised Land. The journey was supposed to start in Egypt and end in Canaan. But Moses came up short. After 40 years of walking in circles, he ended up dying in the desert along with an entire generation of Israelites.

And the Israelites? They grumbled the whole way—all two million of them. "We have no food or water." "We're going to die in the desert." "We were better off as slaves in Egypt." "Moses is never coming down off that mountain." "Let's worship a golden calf!"

Then there's my personal favorite: "When are we going to get to the Promised Land? Are we there yet? Are we there yet? Are we there yet?"

Moses sure didn't have much of a crew. Sometimes I wonder what would have happened if he had a dream team of navigators, military strategists and combat soldiers. Maybe with a crew like that, Moses and the Israelites would have made it to the Promised Land. They could have died fat and happy, gorging on milk and honey under a palm tree in Canaan.

Wouldn't that have been awesome? I wonder.

In 1801, President Thomas Jefferson conceived a similar expedition. Not to the Holy Land, but to a land also thought to be the manifest destiny of its people—the western two-thirds of the United States of America. At that point in time, no man had ever crossed the North American Continent. Jefferson wanted to find out if it was possible, especially whether an all-water access route connected the Atlantic and Pacific Oceans. And he wanted to discover what lay west of the Mississippi River. Prehistoric animals? Savage Indians? The Lost Tribe of Israel? All were popular theories of the day.[98]

For an expedition of this magnitude, no ordinary team of explorers would suffice. It would have to be a dream team.

Captain Meriwether Lewis was the perfect choice to lead the expedition. He was a true renaissance man. A military officer and a frontiersman, he was an expert in hunting, fishing, weapons, tactics, navigation and survival. He was educated in astronomy, medicine, plants and animals. Most importantly, he was a leader of men. For his second officer, Lewis selected William Clarke, whose resumé was only slightly less impressive than his own. Together they hand-picked a crew of the finest young men the nation had to offer.

And on July 5, 1803, the Lewis and Clarke expedition set off on its journey into the great unknown.

The expedition took more than three years from start to finish. By all accounts, it was a rousing success. The journals from the expedition tell of amazing encounters with Indians, astonishing discoveries of new plant and animal species,

---

[98] Stephen E. Ambrose, *Undaunted Courage* (New York: Simon & Schuster, 1996).

harrowing dangers and narrow escapes. But the hardest part of the journey was the discovery that there is no all-water access across the country. Rather, the rivers are separated by a topographical feature, the likes of which they scarcely could have imagined—the Rocky Mountains.

September 16, 1805 was perhaps the worst day of the expedition. The team was deep in the mountains, the snow was heavy, and it was freezing. Nearing starvation, the men began to eat their horses. Whenever they thought it couldn't get worse, it got worse. But somehow they made it through. They made it to the Pacific Ocean. And back. They were heroes.

But none more than Lewis. He had led a team of men on an impossible journey and succeeded. He did what no man had done before—he crossed the entire North American continent. And he captured the imagination of the country in the process. Extravagant receptions were thrown in Lewis' honor. He was appointed Governor of the Louisiana Territory. He could have had anything he desired.

So what did he do? On October 11, 1809, Meriwether Lewis killed himself. He was just 34.

Historians don't know why he did it, but I have a theory. I think that when Lewis ran out of challenges, he ran out of reasons to live. The only thing worse than the Rocky Mountains was not having them anymore. The best part of Lewis' life wasn't completing his journey—it was the journey.

Pastor Andy Stanley says that "when your memories exceed your dreams, the end is near." Those words certainly proved true for Lewis.

Which brings me back to Moses. What a waste. Such a disappointment.

Or was he?

Sure, there was that matter of drawing water from a rock and then taking the credit.[99] In God's eyes, it was a transgression serious enough to preclude Moses from entering the Promised Land. Yet Moses is regarded as the greatest prophet that Israel has ever known (at least until Christ). He was God's hand-picked leader to free the Nation of Israel from 400 years of slavery. He was an instrument for countless miracles. He was ordained to receive and administer God's holy law. He recorded the first five books of the Bible. And he led the Israelites to the gates of the Promised Land.

But more than any of his accomplishments, Moses spoke with God the Father face to face—"as a man speaks with his friend."[100] Imagine having a friendly conversation with the Great I Am!

---

[99] Numbers 20:9-12.
[100] Exodus 33:11.

All that and more happened on Moses' long journey in the desert. It was in the desert that Moses was transformed from a stuttering shepherd into a national leader. It was in the desert that God molded Moses' character. It was in the desert that God taught Moses courage and wisdom and humility. And it was in the desert that Moses became friends with God.

It was in the same desert that the children of Israel completely missed the boat. Like Moses, they were in the very presence of God. Not once, but daily. God appeared to them in a pillar of cloud by day and in a pillar of fire by night. They heard God's voice. They saw manna fall from heaven. They saw the mountain tremble when Moses received the Ten Commandments. They saw miracle after miracle.

And all they could ask was "Are we there yet?"

Moses didn't miss it though. He understood he was given the greatest gift imaginable. To be in the presence of God. To be used by God. To be a friend of God. Moses knew he had arrived at his destination from the first moment he heard God call his name.

Moses lived to the ripe old age of 120. Even then "his eyes were not weak nor his strength gone."[101] Even then, God had one more surprise

---

[101] Exodus 34:7.

in store for him. God told Moses to climb to the top of Mount Nebo. Then God spoke to him one last time: "This is the land I promised on oath to Abraham, Isaac and Jacob . . . I have let you see it with your own eyes . . ."[102] I imagine Moses had tears of joy rolling down his cheeks as he breathed his last breath, the image of the Promised Land dancing before his eyes.

Moses never stepped foot in Canaan, but he went to his reward completely spent, completely satisfied. He fought the good fight. He kept the faith. He finished he race. Moses didn't need a dream team. He had God. And he discovered the greatest of all truths. The goal isn't arriving at any particular destination. It's meeting God on the journey.

Meeting God on the Journey

So Cameron, just how do we meet God? He sure doesn't speak to me like he spoke to Moses. But I do know someone with whom he speaks regularly—your mother.

Kat seems to find God everywhere she looks. Not just in the Bible and in prayer, but in dragon flies that land on her shoulder. In beetles whose eyes light up at night. In summer rain showers and the rainbows that follow. In clouds the shape of

---

[102] Exodus 34:4.

hearts, or angels or Jesus. She says God is showing off just for her.

And it's not just nature where she finds God. God speaks to her in music, in books, in photographs. In odd coincidences and chance encounters that seem to occur daily.

But mainly she's sees the spirit of God in people. She's sees him in the homeless guy on the street corner. In children. In her friends. In you and me. She sees God in times of great joy and profound sadness. She sees him in every situation and every circumstance. God seems to be hovering all around her.

All along Kat's journey, she finds God. It's like she's tuned in to a special frequency. If you asked her though, she'd say that God is all around each of us. He's speaking all the time. If we just pay attention, we might be surprised. He speaks even in the boring things that make up everyday life. Especially in the boring things.

The Boring Things

The 2009 computer-animated movie *Up*[103] is the story of Carl Fredricksen, a shy 8-year-old boy who meets an outgoing girl named Ellie. They

---

[103] *Up*, written by Bob Peterson and Andrew Stanton, directed by Pete Docter (Pixar Animations Studios 2009).

both love adventures. Ellie confides in Carl that her dream is to move her clubhouse, a dilapidated home, to Paradise Falls in South America. Carl and Ellie eventually marry, restore the clubhouse and move in. Over the next 70 years, they save for their trip to Paradise Falls, but life always seems to get in the way of their plans. Just as they finally seem to be able to take their trip, Ellie gets sick and dies. They were never able to have children, so Carl is left all alone. He becomes bitter. All he can think about is his wife.

Out of desperation, Carl comes up with a scheme to keep his promise to Ellie. He ties 10,000 helium balloons to his house. The house begins to float, and Carl is off on his adventure! After a harrowing journey with several plot twists, Carl eventually pilots his house to Paradise Falls—just like Ellie would have wanted.

I love the next scene when Carl settles into his easy chair, the falls in full view right outside his window. Finally, he's arrived at his destination. Now what? Carl doesn't quite know what to do with himself now that his journey is over. Just then he discovers the adventure scrapbook that Ellie had been keeping all those years. Carl thought the pages were left blank for their planned adventure at Paradise Falls. Instead, he discovers that the book is filled with photographs and mementos of their married life together. Nothing extraordinary, just the boring things that make a life.

And on the last page of the scrapbook, Ellie left a final note for Carl. She thanked him for the adventure of their marriage and encouraged him to start an adventure of his own.

As it turns out, the adventure had little to do with the destination. The adventure was in the journey getting there. It was in the seemingly boring things that make up life. That was paradise.

How often do we miss the adventure all around us by focusing on the destination? We keep expecting that our luck will turn. Eventually, things will be just great. But what if this is as good as it gets? What if this is the only paradise this side of heaven?

As Good as it Gets

9/16/06

Cam,

We had a great trip over Labor Day at Riverbend, our mountain cabin in North Carolina. It has 20 acres directly on the river, and it's about the prettiest place in the world. I've been dreaming of owning a place like it since I was a little boy. It was a lifelong dream. And now we have it.

Several friends joined us on the trip. Mike and Jen and their daughter Alexandra. Win and Stephanie and their kids Jackson and Blythe. Even though we had a full-house, you lobbied for your friend Zach to come. We gave in, of course. Zach flew up by himself, so we had to drive back to the Charlotte airport to pick him up. It was a seven-hour roundtrip; we didn't get back to Riverbend until after midnight. But it was worth it. You were so excited to have your buddy with you.

Everyone had a great time. We hiked Stone Mountain. We canoed the New River. Mom was goofing around and tipped her canoe, dumping herself, Win and little Jackson into the river. Thankfully, they all survived (except for Mom's camera). I'm sure Jackson will forever remember it as the day he almost drowned.

Back at the cabin, we road ATV's, played in the river, chopped wood and cooked out—the usual Riverbend stuff. One night we built a bonfire down by the river and roasted hot dogs. We told stories and laughed. As the sun was setting and everyone's face was aglow from the fire, I thought to myself that this was a dream come true. But I just couldn't leave well enough alone. I started talking about my grand plans to buy and develop additional property along the river.

Just as I was really getting into it, Win said something I'll never forget. "Spencer, no matter how many properties you own, you'll never be happier than you are right now."

I've thought about that comment many times since that evening. Right now, we all have our health. We're all together as a family. We're all pursuing worthwhile goals. We're happy. Win was right—this may be as good as it gets.

The day is coming, Cameron, when you will leave the house and go off to college. In a way, all of the days of your life are leading to that one day. When it comes, I'm sure we'll have mixed emotions. We'll be proud of you for making it that far. And we'll be profoundly sad that things will never be the same.

Until that day comes, I'm going to enjoy every minute of our time together. The big things and the little things, the exciting things and the boring things. All things that make up life.

This may be as good as it gets this side of heaven.

Dad

The Adventure of Life

So that's the final lesson, Cameron. You used to ask "are we there yet?" The answer is yes. We've been there the whole time.

This is it. This is life. This is the awesome adventure of life.

Life isn't about the destination. It's about the journey. It's about our gradual but continual refinement toward the perfection of Christ. Never getting all the way there, but making steady progress toward the goal.

At the end of your days, it's the boring things you'll remember. All the little things that make up life. Don't take them for granted. Cherish them. It's like John Lennon said, "Life is what happens when you're busy making other plans."[104]

---

[104] *Beautiful Boy*, written by John Lennon (1980), *Double Fantasy album*.

And please, don't delay joy by engaging in "when and then thinking." Trust me, if you weren't happy on the journey, you won't be any happier when you reach your destination. The reward is the journey.

It's important to celebrate the past and to dream big dreams for the future. I hope you do both. But don't forget to embrace the present. That's where life happens, in the present.

Most importantly, I hope you meet God on your journey. He's always there—you just need to notice.

Now that you've heard all my lessons, Cameron, it's time for you to start your own adventure. Tomorrow isn't promised to any of us, so seize the day.

And always remember to fight the good fight.

Epilogue

I learned so many things in the course of writing this book. Three stand out.

First, I thought I was writing it mainly for you, Cameron. As it turns out, it was as much for me. When you write down what you believe, something happens to you. Your actions become focused and deliberate. At times, I wasn't sure if I was writing the book, or the book was writing me.

Second, I didn't intend to rely so heavily on the Bible. I thought I would just write a few pearls of wisdom I've picked up on my journey. But I couldn't get away from the Bible. I discovered that all real wisdom is based on God's principles.

Third, it took exactly one year to write the book, and I couldn't wait to finish. Now that I'm done, I miss it. Life really isn't about the destination. It's the journey.